PHILIP BARTON

DAWN OF GOLD
THE REAL STORY OF MONEY

ECHO BOOKS

First published in 2015 by Barrallier Books Pty Ltd,
trading as Echo Books.

Registered Office: 35-37 Gordon Avenue, West Geelong, Victoria 3220,
Australia

www.echobooks.com.au

National Library of Australia Cataloguing-in-Publication entry

Creator: Barton, Philip, 1946- author

Title: Dawn of gold : the real story of money/Philip Barton

ISBN: 9780992588076 (hardback)

Dewey Number: 332.4

Cover design by Trinidad James.
Book design and layout by Peter Gamble, Ink Pot Graphic Design, Canberra.
Set in Garamond Premier Pro Display, 12/17 Hype-regular and
Minerva Small Caps.

www.echobooks.com.au

CONTENTS

About the Author

Philip Barton was born in Bushey, England in 1946. In 1965 he departed on what was intended to be a six-month trip and, in his own words, is 'a little overdue back home.'

Since leaving the UK, he has lived in Australia, Colombia, Malaysia, the US and Austria. He has played guitar in a rock band, panned for Gold and worked as a spray-painter, cook, farmer, hat-maker, retailer, lecturer and investor. His interest in Gold spans almost forty years.

Philip Barton is president of the Gold Standard Institute.

Acknowledgements

To my wonderful wife and children who have always tolerated my intense and obsessive exploration of ideas.

To Gaetano Elnekave who, while introducing me to Treviso, Venice and Prosecco wine, gave me the necessary encouragement to kick-start the writing process.

To the fine people of the Gold Standard Institute who have helped me over the years ... particularly Keith Weiner and Rudy Fritsch.

To Professor Antal E. Fekete who kindled my interest in the subject of money and was my first teacher.

To Thomas Bachheimer, the Vienna based Gold and oil trader, and President of the Gold Standard Institute in Europe, who questioned me about 'Gold as a good' (over large glasses of good Viennese beer). The conversation began an invaluable thought process.

To Dick Seegers of Edelmetaal who proofed the book and buoyed me in the final stretch.

INTRODUCTION

Simple can be harder than complex: You have to work hard to
get your thinking clean to make it simple. But it's worth it in
the end because once you get there, you can move mountains.

Steve Jobs

This book was begun with the assumption that Gold is money. Bearing in mind the history of the last 6,000 years that seemed entirely reasonable. The idea was to explore the origins of money and to present a wide-ranging 'Gold For Beginners'—the story of money from its origins, up to its use and implications in the present day.

Outsiders imagine the Gold-money camp as a meeting place for those with the same or similar ideas, an easy uniformity of worldview, a commonality of understanding as to Gold's past, present and future. Not a bit of it. Overnight experts mouth banalities to spellbound audiences of hundreds, sometimes thousands. Ideas for Gold-based monetary systems, ranging from poorly conceived to hopelessly eccentric, circulate the Internet, each with its own enthusiastic camp followers.

There is little agreement. From the most insignificant economic minutia to the widest ranging philosophy, the whole subject area is like the arena of a Roman Circus where, having run short of lions, Gold gladiators are thrown in to fight it out amongst themselves. Rather than uniting and leaping the barricade, they hew and hack at each other without regard for reason and common sense, let alone good manners. It may be impossible to tarnish Gold, but it has not been for lack of trying.

Having grown rather weary at the constancy of how wrong everyone else was, I donned my battle armour, placed a propeller on the top of my cap and joined the fray. What fell out the other side after almost four years of furious laptop tapping was not the book that I had planned. The momentum of the story had moved it into a different dimension of understanding. The story became bogged in two places, which caused almost a year of delay. On both occasions I came to realise that I had been trying to force the story to conform to preconceived ideas of where I knew it should go. It would not. The book progressed when I followed the logic instead of trying to lead it.

This book was not written to plod well-trod ground. The known history of the world has shown quite clearly and undeniably that Gold, in conjunction with silver, works. It has also shown, equally clearly and undeniably, that nothing else does. This book sets out to show why that is so, not that it is so. Others have already done that latter job admirably.

The unveiling of money's origin was a Eureka moment—there turned out to be others. I mulled over new ideas at 2am, 3am, 4am, 5am, then arose invigorated to continue on the trail.

The book addresses some areas that have been improperly or incompletely understood, and others that have not been understood at all. Some years ago I wrote about the importance of Gold's stock-to-flow ratio and received much positive feedback from around the world. Others have subsequently written on the subject and its importance to the Gold as money story[*]. This concept is inspected more closely.

When I began to study money, I was surprised to find that the word had no definition that made sense. Dictionaries are vague on the subject, devoting

---

[*]   In almost all cases making it unduly complicated.

the space to a description of what money does, rather than what money is. The idea of studying something that lacked a coherent definition seemed a dubious proposition.

The starting point for the book became that the definition of money is 'a store of stable value'. Not only did this seem to be Gold's strongest virtue, it is the loss of this quality that causes non-Gold monies to fail. It would either clarify and explain subsequent phenomena and be right, or lead to ever more confusing imponderables and be wrong. Building on a premise is like the construction of an office block; it rests on foundations that will see it either reach a peak of elegant simplicity, or collapse into a rubble of confusion.

———⸎———

The word 'economics' comes from *Eikonomos*—a treatise by Aristotle. It means the science of household management. The basic rule of household management, which is no different from the management of a business or a country, is that one must spend less than one makes. Not the same, and not more, but less, for money must always be set aside for emergencies. The very essence of economics is spending less than one makes while building reserves. The notable thing about reserves is that the prudence displayed in their accumulation means that they are rarely needed. Conversely, those who do not build reserves are precisely the people (or nations) who are rendered destitute by their absence.

It is nonsense to suggest that only economists with a degree are qualified to speak about the economy. Economics and money are not pie-in-the-sky academic abstractions; they are subjects with day-to-day relevance for everyone. The willingness to leave the subject to ivory tower theorists with no experience of wealth creation has had dire consequences that are beginning to manifest.

The remaking of the world to suit the distorted paradigm of modern economic theory is in the process of destroying societies. Paper money is collapsing. Unless we change course, the extreme of this process will see a world that will no longer be able to exchange goods and services and all hell will break loose. The toppling of governments and their replacement, while providing a temporary warm glow, cannot prevent the unfolding of this process. The root cause is an artificial and unsustainable monetary system. This cannot be fixed by legislating around the edges.

It is time for the people to have their say on the subject of money. This book is offered as one contribution to the discussion.

The best method for establishing a valid story is the sequential structuring of events—facts—one after the other. A diligent enough assembly of facts will begin to tell its own story without any need for the author to interrupt. This is not only desirable, but, in most subject areas, also possible. With the origins of Gold, the known facts are sparse and layered with the dust of the ages. Author interruption, otherwise known as speculation, though regrettable, became necessary in parts. The story of Gold begins before written records.

I have tried to avoid too many footnotes. The Internet enables anyone to check what is stated. I have steered clear wherever possible of technical terms. It is not necessary to be an economist or a monetary scientist to understand the origins, mechanics and ramifications of money. Both these bodies have a tendency to make things overly complicated. Having said that, it will be necessary for the reader to think in parts. That was unavoidable.

The intention has been to simplify as far as possible. When a truth is understood, it is always simple ... and obvious. Truth is the ultimate beauty; it adorns the best of humanity and gives sparkle to the nature of existence itself. Truth is the White Knight that gallops out of the golden dawn to slay the dragons of superstition, incompetence and error.

> 'The first duty of a man is the seeking after and the investigation of truth.'
>
> Cicero

Chapter One
Some Gold Nuggets

Har qatl di e jar—zan zamin zar
(Three things for which we kill—land, women and gold)

Pashtun saying

Gold:

Chemical element symbol, Au.
Atomic number, 79.

The story is best begun with an understanding of the properties of Gold and some general knowledge. A century has passed since Gold was on the lips of all people and what was once commonplace is now unknown to many.

'Au' is derived from the Latin word *aurum* meaning 'shining dawn'. It is related to Aurora—the Roman Goddess of the sunrise. Aurora rode into the world in her chariot just ahead of the Sun to announce the dawn of each new day ... much in the manner of the Egyptian Sun God Ra on his Golden barge.

The wondrous metal that is the subject of this book was likely born in the emission of heat and energy that comes about from a supernova ... the explosion of a star. It happens with such unimaginable force that the star is reduced to dust particles. The evidence is that our galaxy has seen at least two supernovas in its history. Many of our ancestors regarded Gold as the physical manifestation of the Sun God on Earth. If Gold does come about as a result of a supernova, they were quite literally correct[*].

———∞∞∞———

Gold is the only 'yellow' metal and, because of this distinction, probably the first metal discovered. It was certainly the first metal noted in the ancient texts. The word 'Gold' traces back to the Old English word *ghel/ghol* and *geolo*, the source of the English 'yellow'. Many languages of the world have the same base formation for the word 'Gold', demonstrating the antiquity of humanity's obsession with this metal.

———∞∞∞———

Gold is the most geologically dispersed of minerals. It has been found on every continent, including Antarctica. It exists in vast quantities in the oceans.

Gold is non-magnetic and neither rusts nor tarnishes. It is almost indestructible. It has been salvaged from wrecks that have been immersed in seawater for two thousand years in the same condition as when the ship first went down. Nitric acid, which can dissolve silver and other metals, has no effect on Gold. Aqua Regia, a highly corrosive acid consisting of three parts hydrochloric to one part nitric, is one of the only substances that can dissolve Gold—neither acid will dissolve Gold on its own[**].

Small quantities of Gold are consumed in industrial applications. It is used as a conductor in situations of extremes of temperature and is the most

---

[*]   The best explanation for the process of Gold formation is contained in an article written by nuclear astrophysicist Dr. Anton Wallner in the December 2013 edition of the monthly journal of the Gold Standard Institute—www.goldstandardinstitute.net. It is in the journal archives for those who are interested.

[**]   A sodium-cyanide solution is another. About 80% of all Gold mined today uses this method. The generally low ore grades remaining (as little as 10grams per tonne of ore) and the cheapness of the sodium-cyanide method have seen it used for around 100 years.

reliable of electrical connections. This has led to its use in the vital area of spacecraft technology. It is also an ideal conductor in minute circuitry. Because pure Gold reflects infrared it is used on the visors of astronauts. The space capsule that carried Neil Armstrong to the Moon's surface was coated with Gold. Its non-corrosion ensures that all cell phones and other electronic devices contain microscopic amounts. Cell phones contain around 25mg [***] of Gold—too little to be worthwhile salvaging.

Gold's reflective qualities are unparalleled. Large new buildings sometimes have Gold particles in their windows. This reflects the heat away during the summer and reflects it inward during the winter, thus providing significant energy savings. Being non-toxic and almost inert, Gold is used by dentists for false teeth, and by surgeons for certain medical procedures. The highest concentration of Gold in the human body is in the region of the heart.

Gold is the most ductile of metals. Though it sounds a bit of a stretch, one single ounce of Gold can be drawn into a wire 50 miles (over 80 kilometres) in length and just 5 microns [****] wide. Gold is also the most malleable of metals. It can be beaten so thin that sunlight can pass through it. One ounce of Gold can be flattened out to create a sheet 100-foot (30 metres) square and five millionth of an inch thick.

The quantities of Gold used for industrial purposes are insignificant in comparison to that which is stored in the form of bullion, coins and jewellery.

———⊗———

Gold and silver deposits are often found together. For this reason, some of the earliest 'Gold' pieces are actually electrum ... a natural mixture of Gold and silver. The earliest Gold-workers were unable to separate the

---

[***]   A milligram (mg) is one thousandth of a gram, or one millionth of a kilogram.

[****]   A micron is a millionth of a metre.

two metals. For a long time it was believed the original electrum coin from Lydia (circa 650 B.C.) was due to this factor. More recent research suggests that the proportion of silver to Gold in the Lydian coin was unlikely to have occurred naturally.

This duller coloured electrum was the original 'white Gold', though if the silver content is high enough it will produce a greenish tinge. Today, 'white Gold' is more normally Gold mixed with zinc, nickel, manganese or palladium. Coloured Gold can be obtained by alloying (mixing) with other metals. Blue Gold is Gold mixed with iron; purple Gold is Gold mixed with aluminium. Red, rose and pink Gold are made by alloying Gold with differing amounts of copper. Most jewellery and coins contain a small amount of copper to give the Gold added strength. Without the copper and when warm, Gold is so soft it can be marked with a tooth.

In the smaller quantities, Gold is usually measured in grams or troy ounces. Troy ounces are slightly heavier than the avoirdupois ounce of the kitchen.

The origin of 'troy' in the context of Gold ounces comes from the town of Troyes in Champaign, France. The Troyes fair dates back to at least the 5th century AD and by the 13th century had evolved into a significant centre of commerce. At the time Troyes vied with Paris as the most important town in France. As with most other markets, it used its own system of weights and measures. Because Troyes was famous and attracted merchants from many other countries, the use of its ounces as a unit of weight spread far and wide.

Troy ounces were used to weigh a variety of products including grain, but today are used only to weigh Gold, silver, platinum and gunpowder. The exact weight of a troy ounce is reputed to have arrived from the Indus Valley via the Romans.

Weight conversions:

1 troy ounce = 480 grains
1 troy ounce = 31.1 grams
1 kilo =   32.15 troy ounces
1 tonne =   32,150.75 troy ounces
1 tonne =   1,000,000 grams
1 tonne =   15,432,358 grains

Different parts of the world traditionally use differing weight measures for Gold. The international weight is the gram. The regional weights are:

		Grams
Troy ounce	Anglo countries	31.10
Tola	India and Middle East	11.66
Tael	Hong Kong and Taiwan	37.43
Tael	China	50.00
Don	South Korea	3.75
Chi	Vietnam	3.75
Baht	Thailand	14.71

The Gold content of jewellery is measured in karats (or carats). The word is derived from the carob seed, which was believed to have a uniform weight of 200mg. This led to its use as a counterweight by ancient merchants in what we know today as the Middle East. The reality is that the carob seed, whilst having an average weight of about 200mg, has as much variation in weight as most other seeds.

There appears to be a long history of a weight carrying a name associated with carob and with a mass close to that of a single carob bean. For example, the ancient Greeks had a small weight, the kerat, while the siliqua (from the Latin for carob, siliqua Graeca) is the smallest subdivision (1/1728) of the Roman pound[*****]. Incidentally, the measure of gold purity—also called the carat (UK English) or karat (US English)—derives from the time of the Emperor Constantine when a new gold coin was struck at 72 to the Roman pound, meaning that each coin weighed 24 siliquae or carats[******].

[*****]   Smith, W. 1870 *Dictionary of Greek and Roman Antiquities*. Boston: Little & Brown

[******]   Turnbull et al. (2006). *Biology Letters*, **2**, 397-400

Karats no longer refer to weight, but to purity. Pure Gold is 24 karats (24k). When a Gold bracelet is described as 18 karats, it means that 18 parts out of the 24 are pure Gold and the other 6 parts are alloy. So the higher the number, the closer it approaches the pure Gold state of 24 karats. Gold jewellery is rarely made out of pure Gold because without an alloy it is too soft and is subject to wear and damage. 22k jewellery is common in India where Gold continues to be regarded as money, but 18k is the highest generally available elsewhere.

The purest form of available Gold today is 0.99999. This means that it is 99.999% pure. 24k Gold is any purity at 99.00% or above.

Gold %	European System	Karat System
99+	990	24k
91.6	916	22k
75	750	18k
58.5	585	14k
41.7	417	12k

Generally speaking bullion and coins are described in decimal terms, while jewellery is described in karats. The decimal measure of fineness is now creeping into the sphere of jewellery also and it could be speculated that the long and distinguished, though somewhat mythical, history of the karat in reference to Gold is drawing to a close.

—⊶⊷—

The Olympic Gold medal was truly that until 1912. Today, an Olympic Gold medal has 6 grams of Gold in it. As the weight of an Olympic Gold medal is 250 grams that means the Gold content is 2.4%. With the amount of money generated from the Olympics it seems inappropriate and in poor taste to short-change the winners with such an adulterated token. A jeweller would not consider that the medal should be labelled 'Gold' with such a small quantity involved.

An average human body contains approximately 0.2 mg of Gold. The concentration of Gold in the human body is denser than in the oceans.

There is more Gold residing in the bodies of the average crowd at an Olympic event than there is in the medal that the winner receives.

—⚬⚬⚬—

The word 'Gold' has come to symbolise not only the metal itself, but anything associated with value, wealth, standing, excellence, purity, royalty and prestige. From Gold credit cards, Gold records, Gold ratings and 'Golden years', through to Gold stars for 'top of the class' school children.

The ultimate expression for something of superior quality is that it is as 'good as Gold'. A wonderful person is 'worth their weight in Gold' or they may have a 'heart of Gold'. A person who woos someone purely for his or her money is a 'Gold digger'. An age of prosperity and peace is a 'Golden age'. A distant or imaginary reward is known as a 'pot of Gold'.

The Incas regarded rainbows as a gift from the Sun God. Iris was the Greek goddess of the rainbow that was considered a path between the Earth and Heaven. Due to the obvious connection of a rainbow to the Sun, these and similar beliefs, are the source of the delightful story of Gold being located at the base of a rainbow.

Gold is money, and has been for 3,500 years. Most of the Gold ever mined is still available for use. It is constantly being melted down and reworked into new shapes. The likelihood is that the Gold ring on your finger contains particles of the same Gold that adorned an Egyptian pharaoh. There is a continuity to Gold that parallels the continuity of humanity itself.

CHAPTER TWO
EXISTING THEORIES

*There are two mistakes one can make along the road to
truth—not going all the way, and not starting.*

Buddha

What is money? The answer isn't taught in schools, it isn't taught
anywhere. Ten economists will give ten different answers, all of them
vague. The money of our planet is no better understood than the dark
matter of space.

Today we use paper and base metal coins as money. Government
experiments with paper money have come and gone with great regularity
over the last thousand years. In recent centuries, despots such as Napoleon,
Lenin, Hitler and Mao Zedong were swept to power on the back of the
social destruction brought about by the collapse of their nation's paper
monies. Far too much attention has been paid to the philosophies that
these people promoted, rather than the grim monetary circumstances
that made people desperate enough to listen.

Paper money has a dismal track record.

⸻ ⊗⊗⊗ ⸻

One hundred years after Gold was withdrawn from circulation in 1914,
central banks still keep a major portion of their reserves in Gold. In 2013

they again began adding to those reserves. Other materials, including seashells, leather coins, beads and paper, have been tried as money, but they always eventually fail. Only Gold has stood the test of time, but why—what is so unique about Gold?

The answer lies not in the present, but at the beginnings of human society. The extraordinary occurrence that eventually led humanity to money happened around the time that people first began to congregate and to contemplate the nature of the universe.

Ultimately, Gold is money because the people of the world agree that it is. It therefore becomes important to discover the foundation of this agreement. What does it rest on—where did it come from? Why is it that when government imposed monetary systems break down, which has been regularly and reliably happening since at least the 3rd century AD, the world always returns to Gold? We have missed something crucial to our understanding of money. Yet it has lain in plain view for 6,000 years and has been noted in a wide body of literature. It was not the fact that was overlooked, just its significance.

———⧙⧘———

There are two existing theories on the origins of money. 'Gift Economics' maintains that barter economies are a myth and that people gave things away in the expectation of being given something back of similar worth in the future; a crude system of credit. Observation and the success of eBay bears witness to the dubiousness of this theory. If it were a basic human action to produce surplus goods in order to give them away for the possibility of future return, then it would be evident to this day. It is not.

Such tenuous support as there is for the theory is claimed to come from the failure to find the physical locations where barter happened. There is a simple explanation for that. By its nature barter was rarely a centralised endeavour. Barter is the direct exchange of goods and has been happening since long before the evolvement of societies, or even primitive villages. To suggest it never happened in centralized locations however is shown false by tomb scenes from the Egyptian 4th Dynasty. They depict people exchanging commodities, one against the other—fish, fishhooks, fans, necklaces etc.

That there are situations and times when people give things away is observably true, but that a theory of the origins of money can be arrived at from such observations is not. The occurrence of someone giving away something of perceived value is associated with great love or friendship, ceremonial bonding such as weddings, a wish to support a worthy cause, intimidation or a desire to ingratiate. These situations have no bearing on commercial transactions.

None of this is to deny that complex systems of credit have been around for at least 6,000 years. A basic form of credit would have emerged at the same time as barter ... 'Can I borrow some nuts? I'll give them back tomorrow'. It was circa 3,200 BC in Mesopotamia that the first levelling out mechanism to balance the books is recorded. It was called the Shekel and stood for a weight of grain. It is stretching a long bow past breaking point to surmise from this that grain became money. As will become clear, a perishable cannot be money.

The theory of gift economics is a recycling of the deservedly obscure speculations of a German economist named Georg Friedrich Knapp*. Knapp believed that money was an abstract institution created by governments. The idea has never gained much traction. It is not in the nature of governments to invent or develop anything, certainly nothing as sensible and useful as money.

The second and more plausible theory is that money arose as the logical extension of barter. This was the view of Carl Menger and is examined in more detail later in the book.

---

*   The State Theory of Money 1905.

---⊗∞⊗---

A valid theory on the origin of money would have to resolve the problems of money not only in the past, but also in the present. It would have to resolve the age-old mystery of the origins and nature of the relationship between Gold and silver. It would explain why only the two monetary metals have succeeded as money over the longer term. It would serve to clarify the monetary science by resolving the existing disagreements that cause endless debate. It should allow us to at once know whether something was a valid money, or, and just as importantly, whether it was not. It would mean that money was no longer cloaked in dark economic terms, but could stand in the bright light of common sense.

Menger's observation that barter led to some goods being more popular in trade than others (goats, cows, salt, seeds, grain etc.) is obviously and undeniably true, but that had no bearing on the origin of money. Surprisingly, money's origin had nothing to do with the exchange of goods in the marketplace.

Not so surprisingly, it was far removed from a government legislative process.

---⊗∞⊗---

On February 17th, 2000, the economist and chairman of the US Federal Reserve Bank, Alan Greenspan, stated in front of Congress:

'We have a problem trying to define exactly what money is ... '

How could there be a valid school of economics that did not have a sound knowledge of money—that could not even define it? How could it be that at the start of the 21st century the world could have reached the bizarre point of having the man who was in charge of the U.S. Federal Reserve Bank, the most powerful monetary force in the world, concede that he did not understand money? It is beyond debate that there can be no real understanding of any subject when the subject itself lacks a correct definition.

The book begins with the theory that money is defined: 'a store of stable value'. The book will progress from that—or not.

—∞∞∞—

Gold speaks to the integrity of humanity. Gold is not only the foundation of all wealth and societies, it also murmurs to the greed that tempts the darker recesses of the soul. After procreation, sustenance, shelter and basic communication, Gold has the most universal demand. At the beginning of the 21st century, generations have come and gone who have never used Gold as money; yet still it is highly prized. What is it about Gold that allows it to defy official disdain with impunity? What is the attribute of Gold that has held firm for over 6,000 years and which has existed amongst people in almost every culture and in all parts of the world?

The discovery of the true origins of money stemmed from a study of Gold's 'stock-to-flow ratio'. It is necessary to understand this one simple tool, and its relevance and importance to the story, before going any further.

CHAPTER THREE
THE STOCK-TO-FLOW
RATIO

Truth, like gold, is to be obtained not by its growth, but by washing away from it all that is not gold.

Leo Nikolaevich Tolstoy

If it is true that stability of value is the crux of monetary matters, then an understanding of the stock-to-flow ratio is of supreme importance. If nothing else is gained other than a thorough grasp of this, then the reader will be ahead of most in the Gold community, and way ahead of the vast majority of economists. No valid understanding of Gold can be attained without it. The stock-to-flow ratio is the uncomplicated technical entry point into the subject.

———— ❧ ————

Gold has been used to store wealth for thousands of years. Only a small percentage of Gold has ever been used by industry and much of that is recycled. What this means is that the vast majority of all the Gold ever mined is still available for use. Around 174,000 tonnes is quoted as being the total amount of Gold available in the world. This figure is known as the 'stock'.

Each year about 2,700 tonnes of Gold is mined. This is known as the 'flow'. It is from these two amounts that the ratio is derived. When the stock is divided by the flow (174,000 ÷ 2,700), it produces a stock-to-flow ratio of 64 to 1. The stock-to-flow ratio is a way of stating the total amount of above ground stock, relative to the amount that is being produced by the mines each year. It is no more complicated than that.

What this ratio lacks in complication, it makes up for in importance. The point to hang on to is that the stock of Gold is far, far greater than the amount of new Gold arriving in the market each year. This leads to a situation where the value of Gold is very stable. The larger the Gold stock becomes, the less influenced it is by the flow of Gold from the mines. Having been accumulated for at least 6,000 years, the amount of stock is now so great that Gold's value is uninfluenced by variations in the amount entering the market from the mines each year.

It is this huge amount of stock that gives Gold its stability of value. No other commodity has anywhere near this stock-to-flow ratio *. What this means is that nothing else has Gold's stability of value. Most other commodities have a miniscule stock-to-flow ratio; their stock is less than the yearly flow—almost as fast as they are mined, they are used. World stocks of ordinary commodities are rarely sufficient to last more than a few months.

When there is only a small stock of a commodity compared to flow, then its value can fluctuate enormously. A new large mine would increase the flow and result in a fall in the value of the commodity. A sudden closing of a large mine would increase the value. Volatility in supply would cause instability in the market value of any commodity with a small above ground stock. Because of its high stock-to-flow ratio, Gold holds its value with a stability that is matched by nothing else, and can be matched by nothing else. The stock of Gold is equivalent to 64 years worth of flow. The stock of most other commodities would be depleted 64 *days* after mining ceased.

---

*   Silver also has an unusually large stock-to-flow ratio, though not as large as Gold's

If Gold were just a normal commodity, its value would tumble with 174,000 tonnes already in existence. It is the constancy of the demand for Gold's stability of value that ensures that the stock grows ever larger and, because of that, the value ever more stable—they are mutually reinforcing phenomena. It is Gold's incomparably high stock-to-flow ratio that ensures it is, and will always be, the most stable store of value available. Gold has been accumulated for at least 6,000 years to achieve the stock-to-flow ratio that it has today. How could anything else ever match this?

Platinum Money

Because of its scarcity, it has been suggested that platinum** could be a new monetary metal. But in the event that flow (mining) was to stop, then stocks of platinum would be exhausted in a matter of weeks. In those circumstances the value of platinum would skyrocket. That makes platinum far too volatile for use as money; it can never be a store of stable value because its stock is too small. Platinum is a precious metal; it can never be a monetary metal.

The idea that platinum could be a monetary metal is not new. Platinum coins were minted in Russia under Czar Nicholas 1st. They contained nine parts Gold with sixty-eight parts of 'pure Urals platinum' and were produced at the Saint Petersburg Mint from 1828 to 1845. Apart from being a very difficult to mint coin because of the metal's hardness, they failed to circulate. They were never accepted as money because their value was not stable. The 'platinum for money' proponents have laboured under the common misconception that Gold is money because it is scarce—rare. On the contrary, Gold is money because there is so much of it ... relative to flow.

** The Spanish first discovered platinum in Colombia. They named it *platina*, meaning 'little silver'. It was regarded as a nuisance because it sank to the bottom of the pans along with the Gold and silver.

The logic has been forwarded that much of the Gold stock should not be regarded as such because it is not available right now. That is an argument that serves more to cloud the issue than to clarify it. 'Stock' should not be interpreted as meaning that the whole amount is available to the market at any particular moment in time. All that can be surmised from the phrase 'stock' is that it exists in an available form and could enter the market at any time were its owners so inclined.

Just because something exists, it cannot be assumed that it will be available to the market whenever the market wants it. What it does mean is that it can become available to the market at some point—any point. Opinions as to how likely it is that various entities will put their Gold into the marketplace are just that—opinions. They have no bearing on the designation of all above ground Gold as 'stock'.

Gold follows an inviolable cycle: accumulation—dispersal—accumulation. The Gold is permanent; its whereabouts is not. The owners, seemingly impregnably entrenched during their own era, are inevitably blown away by the winds of time. History exposes them as mere temporary custodians. Where today is the Gold of Egypt that existed for at least 6000 years, or Byzantium or Manichaeism?

———⊗⊗⊗———

It has been assumed that it is wholly the stock-to-flow ratio that gives Gold its stability of value. There is enormous usefulness in understanding the stock-to-flow ratio and its importance to this essential feature of Gold but, despite the compelling logic of the theory, it is not the whole truth. To understand the story of money it is necessary to return right to the beginning.

From the entry point of the stock-to-flow ratio of Gold, we can not only move forward to an understanding of its stability of value and the ramifications and importance of that in the present day, but we can move backward to discover the origins of Gold's importance. The stock-to-flow ratio is pivotal to unlocking the millennia long mystery of Gold and money.

The Beginning

There is a start to everything. A stock of 174,000 tonnes does not just suddenly appear; it is the end result of a long, process of incremental accumulation. At a moment in time, way back at the dawn of human history, the fateful decision was made to begin to accumulate Gold. One person made that decision. Others followed this first unknown and unsung hero.

Yet no one would put aside a dozen eggs or some iron bars and expect them to have value sixty years later, let alone sixty centuries later.

This is a crucial point to understand in the search for the origins of money. The lasting and worldwide agreement to begin to acquire and accumulate Gold informs us that right from the beginning, from the moment the first unrefined nugget was set aside, Gold was already considered a store of stable value. If not, the decision to hoard it would not have been made. Something with an unstable value would not be widely stored. This one step back was the foot in the door of Gold's origins as money.

The Cro-Magnon people (European Early Modern Humans) were among the earliest accumulators. Their Gold, in the form of rough nuggets gathered from where they discovered them in the streams, or just lying on the ground, has been found in their burial sites and cave dwellings dating as far back as 30,000 BC. Crude Gold has been found among the remains of almost all prehistoric people. The earliest discovered large cache of European 'worked' Gold comes from the Varna Necropolis in modern day Bulgaria and is dated circa 4,500 BC. Both the original hoards of nuggets and the jewellery discovered at Varna were for purposes far more significant than decoration.

Gold was not hoarded or worn because it was pretty.

———∞∞∞———

Gold Accumulation Pre-Dated Commercial Use

Two pertinent and closely related points emerge from all this:

1. Gold was accumulated for thousands of years before it was used in the marketplace, which means that,

2. Gold's stability of value was formed before it became money.

These points are of the utmost significance to the unveilings of money's origins. What these overlooked, but indisputable historical facts confirm is that long before its commercial use was understood, Gold was already perceived to be a store of stable value. The primary function of money was formed independent of the exchange of goods. This was the first Eureka moment in the tracking down of money's origins.

> However common money seems to us from our constant use of it, we should consider how good reason our forefathers had to amass it.
>
> Cassiodorus—5th century BC

———∞∞∞———

Gold now has a stock-to-flow ratio, with the consequent stability of value, sufficient to ensure that it will forever remain the only money. But the proper sequence of events must be established if the correct picture is to emerge. Gold did not become a store of stable value because of the stock-to-flow ratio. This reverses cause and effect. Gold gained its high stock-to-flow ratio because it had already attained the status of a store of stable value. Only once this status had been granted did Gold then begin to be accumulated. It was this original status that resulted in the vast stock that exists in the world today.

What was the basis of the stable value that was assigned to Gold and that pre-dated its use in the marketplace by thousands of years?

What caused Gold to be hoarded prior to the emergence of its commercial value? Why has Gold played a central role in every major society throughout the entire history of the world?

What is the real significance of Gold?

CHAPTER FOUR
THE SUN GOD

Night's darkness is the bag that bursts with the gold of the dawn
Rabindranath Tagore

And so the search for the where and the why of the first Gold hoards set off—back to the distant past. The initially somewhat overwhelming puzzle of where to begin the search for a needle in a haystack, was soon replaced by the realization that the needle was everywhere—pinned into the beginnings of all societies.

It was not only the passage of so much time that had obscured the connection; it was also the academic gulf between the study of the history of early societies and the study of money.

Circa 10,000 BC the Great Ice-Age began to recede. At its peak, one third of the planet, including whole valleys and rivers, was covered by ice that in places was thousands of feet thick. The sparse survivors of humankind had eked out a miserable existence by trapping animals ... the meat was eaten and the skins were worn. It was the strongest human males who mated; the offspring had to be hardy ... only the fittest survived. There were few trees and no grass, just shrubs, bushes, moss ... and interminable cold. Lives were dominated by the pressing needs of day-to-day survival. Food and warmth were in short supply.

The estimated human population of planet Earth was just five million.

By 7,000 BC, apart from the mountain peaks and Polar Regions, the ice had gone. Most of the tundra had melted and the glaciers had retreated. The world greened and animal and plant life became more plentiful. Human survival was no longer so precarious. Gradually the skins were shed for lighter garments as the land, air and waters warmed. The unseen forces that had caused the terrible cold, had been defeated by a superior force ... the Sun. That the Sun became worshipped as the dominant deity is a fact; why that was so must forever remain speculative.

Another of the theories for the supremacy of the Sun God is based on the invention of the solar calendar. This is recorded as having happened at Lunu (renamed Heliopolis by the Greeks and known to the Arabs as Ain Shams 'the well of the Sun'), the great Egyptian seat of learning at the mouth of the Nile Delta in Egypt. It superseded the lunar calendar, which though pivotal to the mastery of crop growth and the beginning of the first credibly recorded large-population society, lacked precision. The solar calendar allowed exact predictions to be made on the timing of the annual Nile flooding. The invention of the solar calendar, and its adoption by the Egyptian priesthood, does not explain the almost simultaneous emergence of Sun deification in other parts of the world, but neither can it be dismissed.

The more likely situation is that the creation of the solar calendar in Egypt confirmed the Sun God's already exalted stature.

—— ◦⥾◦ ——

Many of our earliest ancestors, including those of the Indus Valley, the Incan Empire, Egypt, China, Japan, Greece and Persia worshipped the Sun God. No other deity has been worshipped for longer, or by a larger percentage of the population of the world[*]. By the 5th dynasty (circa 2500 BC) Ra, the

[*]   The tradition lingers on with the Dutch, Germans, Norwegians, Swedish, Anglos and others, still observing Sunday, the day of the sun, as their day of religious observance. The day of the Sun is also a part of many other languages such as Cantonese and Thai, though is now devoid of religious observance.

God of the Sun, was the dominant Egyptian deity.

> The soul is the emanation of divine light, represented in material form as the sun. The sun's rays enter the human body at birth and at death return to the eternal deity who is the source of all light. The human life cycle is essentially part of the solar system.
>
> Otto Neubert—*The Valley of the Kings*

It is impossible to overstate the importance of the Sun God to the Ancient Egyptians.

The first Gold nugget was probably plucked out of a stream when someone stopped to drink and noticed a glitter in the water. It would have been an object of wonder. Our earliest ancestors discovered that the 'glitter' was soft and could be moulded into pleasing shapes and designs. In this, or some similar way, Gold entered the rudimentary shelters of our forebears. What did they make of it? They could not have appreciated the significance of the moment; that this beautiful metal would not only influence the future of the human race, but forge it in a way that would have been otherwise inconceivable.

The evidence is quite clear. After an unknowable number of years, Gold came to be regarded as the Earthly manifestation of the Sun God— a divine phenomenon. In Ancient Egypt and China, a circle with a point at its centre was the symbol for both the Sun and Gold.

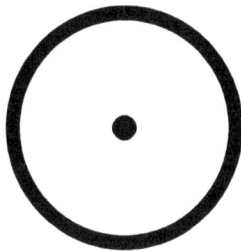

The Sun and Gold were perceived as being at the centre of existence. At least 6,000 years ago, people from various cultures around the world began to accumulate Gold. Without any known means of contact or communication, they nevertheless came to the same belief ... the belief that not only was Gold holy, but that it was the Earthly manifestation of god.

> The shining golden sarcophagi and jewels in the tombs all guaranteed immortality to the deceased because gold was of the same material as the eternal sun.
>
> Hans Wolfgang Müller (Professor of Egyptology at the University of Munich)—*Gold of the Pharaohs*

One of the earliest known geological maps (circa 1300 BC) is a diagram of the Gold mines at Wadi Hammamat in eastern Egypt. The mountains are labelled 'mountains of Gold' and 'mountains of silver and Gold'[**]. The inseparable nature of the concept of god and Gold is made clear by the marking on some of the Gold mountains as 'the peak where Amun is'. Gold was god.

The connection between the Sun and Gold was inevitable. The indestructible nature and brilliance of Gold aligned with the timeless, brilliance of the Sun God. Even the early Greeks posited that Gold was a dense form of sunlight mixed with water. Hieroglyphs dating back to 2,600 BC describe Gold as divine and indestructible.

It is an unambiguous fact that Gold was assigned a deeply spiritual meaning. The reverence that all these early societies bestowed upon Gold can only be appreciated by the understanding that they regarded the Sun as the omnipotent deity, and Gold as the Earthly manifestation of that deity. No other icon has ever attained such stature.

Gold and the concept of god became indivisible.

Gold was a repository of holy value, a value superior to all others. By common agreement, Gold had been elevated to a store of spiritual value that was as stable and eternal as any value could be. It was this decidedly non-commercial stability of value that began the process of Gold hoarding

---

[**]   If this latter translation is correct, it places a large question mark over the commonly held belief that there was not much silver in Egypt.

that would result in the vast stock of Gold available to the world today.

The first recorded intense accumulation of Gold was begun in the Pharaohs' temples to the Sun God.

It was a stability of perception, granted by the stability of representation, which created the world's only stable value. That stability was directly proportional to the strength, consistency and commonality of humanity's spiritual aspirations. Within the consciousness of each and every person resides one common and timeless value: the yearning to understand life at the level that seems to lie just beyond the ability to reason. This urge has preoccupied and driven all the great philosophers and thinkers from the time the first gnarly human foot walked the Earth to the pedicured, well-shod present.

It was this eternal yearning that underpinned the worship of the Sun God and that became symbolised by Gold. It was the stability of this one eternal value that transferred over to Gold and elevated it to the status of god on Earth. Gold was the Sun and the Sun was god. This was the basis of the agreement that Gold was a store of stable value. Though still a spiritual value, the uniqueness of this feature was to have profound and far-reaching consequences.

> The attachment of humans to gold is remarkable; I suspect there is something metaphysical about gold that attracts human beings. Perhaps gold is part of the natural order of things, part of the Rerum Natura, and the relationship of humans to gold is 'built-in' into human nature, like sexual attraction.
>
> Hugo Salinas Price

It was the stable spiritual value assigned to Gold by this representation that brought about the large stock-to-flow ratio. This in turn eventually became the stable temporal value so suited for the marketplace.

The idea that Gold's stability of value, the ultimate tool of commerce, could have derived from a spiritual source was at first glance preposterous. On a personal note, I will admit to a long pause—many months—at this point while I tried to find the error in the logic; some other explanation. It was a far distance from the envisaged direction of the story. Finding no other credible avenue to explore, I persisted.

It is easily demonstrated that the source of Gold's stability was other than the marketplace, because accumulation only happens with a stable value, and the accumulation of Gold preceded marketplace application. If the stability of value was not a marketplace value, then what other value is available?

That Gold is the only store of stable value means that its source is not only unusual, but also probably exclusive. If that were not so, then there likely would be more than one stable value. It also had to be a value that was universal; otherwise Gold would not have arisen as money throughout the world.

The value that most comfortably 'fits the bill' is the spiritual value attached to the worship of the universal god—the Sun God. This spiritual source eventually settled as the prime, though initially very contra-intuitive, candidate.

That Gold was the representative of the Sun God made the 'preposterous' seem more and more plausible. This was no god in the manner of modern gods; an abstract entity sometimes worshipped on Saturdays or Sundays and largely forgotten at other times. The Sun God was at the centre of existence; powerful and omnipresent and guiding each moment of the day and the seasons.

The Sun God was omnipotent and to hold Gold in one's hand was to be in direct touch with god. To be with Gold was to be with god.

———◦∞◦———

Such markets as existed in the ancient societies involved crude credit and barter; in other words, they swapped goods for those that were perceived to be of a same or similar value. Gold was hoarded purely for its sacred value.

The value attached to Gold pre-1500 BC was not a monetary value in accord with today's understanding of the word; they did not yet know what money was. It was, nevertheless, a profound value. It was senior to the modern concept of money and embodied the quest for the one constant that people from all over the world have held for the whole of recorded history. Without that one constant, there never could have been money. From this association of Gold with the Sun God was set in motion a course of monetary events that is now not only unstoppable, but, because of the resultant stock-to-flow ratio, largely independent of its original cause.

This separation of Gold from its deified status does not mean that the relationship has become irrelevant. The knowledge of the true origins of Gold's stability of value parts the clouds of history. As will become evident, it allows access to a clear view of much that had remained incomprehensible.

—❀—

We now have a stock-to-flow ratio sufficient to ensure that Gold continues as not only money, but also the only possible money. However, cause and effect must be clearly understood. It was the value assigned by virtue of Gold's holy bond with the Sun God that underpinned its transition to a store of stable value. It was the hoarding that resulted from this that led to the high stock-to-flow ratio that ensured that, with or without its sacred association, Gold became the one and only money.

What the stock-to-flow ratio of Gold does is not only confirm, but also continue to create Gold's status as a store of stable value. It was not the original cause of that status.

—❀—

Gold took its first step on its grand journey to the marketplace when it became a store of stable spiritual value. This stable value, due to the stability of its representation of the sole constant in human consciousness, is unique. It is only by the understanding of this one crucial factor that the full significance of money itself can be understood.

That stable value is still locked up in every single grain of Gold to this day. Even those who argue against Gold would never be so foolish as to walk past a gram of Gold lying in the road. They may not like the fact that Gold is money, but they know with a certainty as sure as Croesus, that this is precisely what it is.

It needs no legal tender laws to make it desirable[***].

—————⊗⊗⊗—————

That Gold and god were conceptually indivisible is the base that money was built upon. This was the foundation stone for our first societies. The connection between Gold and the spiritual aspirations of our ancestors has been long forgotten, but the significance of that original union will grace all the time for which there is a human history to record.

—————⊗⊗⊗—————

The story of Gold's migration into vast hoards has been an uninspected, part of human history. Even more important, and equally uninspected, was the story of its subsequent exit.

[***]   'Legal tender' carries the legal obligation that it must be accepted if offered in payment of any debt.

CHAPTER FIVE
THE MIRACLE OF CIRCULATION

Soldiers of the pen, soldiers of science. From the tops of these
pyramids fifty centuries of history are looking down on
you. A great task awaits you. The world yearns to know the
history of Egypt. Get to work.

Napoleon Bonaparte 1798
(the beginnings of Egyptology)

Gold's paradigm shift, from a store of stable spiritual value to a store of stable temporal value, took thousands of years. The first recorded manifestation of its commercial application was in Egypt. Once the basic and essential ingredient of money had materialized, why did this progression not happen sooner?

Circa 1550 BC, the Egyptians invaded Nubia (Ta-Nub—'the land of Gold', now known as Northern Sudan) and took over the Gold mines. The Gold had flowed from Nubia to Egypt for an unknowable number of years prior to this, but now it sped up dramatically.

It was not until the Nubian mines started disgorging their huge reserves, that Gold became widely distributed. Originally, Gold had been the preserve of the Pharaohs. It was only later that small amounts became distributed by royal decree. Even then it was restricted to esteemed members of the inner court and priesthood. Eventually this came to include high officials of the empire. The awarding of this 'Gold of Honour' was significant and unusual enough to be recorded on the recipient's tombs. Gold was revered in the same manner as the Sun God and its possession was closely guarded. Gold jewellery was not an adornment, a trinket; it was the mark of the highest stature. Wearing it signified proximity and devotion to god and the chance of immortality.

> It was the land of Pharaoh the 'Horus of gold', the 'god of gold', the king who held the monopoly over the sacred metal.
>
> Rainer Stadelmann—First Director of the German Archaeology Institute, Cairo

Gold's monopolization was common to the rulers of all the ancient Sun cultures. The original hoarding and flaunting of Gold is the likely source of the misconception that Gold was just a symbol of power. Gold symbolized the eternal quest for 'oneness' with God; it was regarded as the spiritual nexus between Earth and the afterlife. This symbolism was most potent in the Egyptian burial chambers and best demonstrated by Tutankhamen's Gold mask. Thus clad he was assured entrance to the Egyptian pantheon.

The Pharaonic burials were not a funeral in the modern sense. This was no place for the grieving of relatives or celebration of the life and times of the occupant. No mention of what a good or bad ruler he may have been; no mention of anything personal at all. The entombment, with the rituals, paintings, objects and other accoutrement was not symbolic; it was functional. The delicate little wall drawings were not art; they were an instruction manual.

The whole structure and performance existed to facilitate the Pharaoh's passage from the world of humans, to the world of gods. Underneath the instructions for the rite of passage lay the one crucial component without which the other steps were not credible ... Gold

That the ownership of Gold was associated with power and stature is indisputable, but that is so today and we do not bury people surrounded by Gold to show it. Such matters are demonstrated in life, not death. These early, overt displays of Gold were designed to show the devotion and worthiness of the owner or, in the case of Tutankhamen's mask, of those about to meet their creator, the very opposite of power.

The Wealth of Egypt

Generalised statements are made about the period prior to the New Kingdom to the effect that Egypt was very rich. This is misleading. The distinction is rarely made between the Pharaonic court and ordinary working people. The working people survived on an allotment of bread and beer while living in mosquito infested mud huts.

The Egyptian Gold was held in the courts and temples and had no commercial significance. The wealth of Egypt was derived from the agricultural bonanza made possible by the yearly flooding of the Nile. The whole economy was in the rigid grip of the Pharaoh and his court and administrators. They controlled the complete structure of society, from trade to land and resources[*]. Commerce among the people was restricted to barter. Outside the ruling class, people possessed neither Gold nor silver. The divine metals were not seen outside the court and had no monetary significance at either end of the huge wealth divide.

This is not to suggest that there was no Gold at all in private hands prior to 1500 BC. The nomads of the Eastern deserts brought small quantities of Gold into the cities and traded with it. Isolated pieces of crudely made religious offerings have been found in the graves of non-court people from circa 3000 BC.

---

[*]   There is no record of any government regulation or management of water. It appears that the Pharaonic courts restricted themselves to the confiscation of wealth; they did not directly meddle in its production. This would explain the continuous nature of the agricultural prosperity and the fact that the Egyptian society was the longest lasting in recorded history.

While access to Gold was not easy, the desire for immortality was just as strong with the Egyptian serfs as it was with the Pharaohs.

The arrival of Gold from Nubia began to change this exclusivity. Reliable records of the tonnage that came out of the mines are not available, but the scribes of the time left no room for doubt that Nubia produced Gold in unusually large amounts. The Gold that had been the preserve of a select few began to be spread more widely; finally it reached the marketplace. Prior to the emergence of Gold with its unique property, the marketplace, as we know it today, did not, could not, exist. Without a broadly available store of stable value, there was no possibility of a widespread and easy exchange of goods and services.

By 1500 BC, Gold had already been accumulated in Egypt for at least 2,500 years without any appreciable quantities making it into the hands of the people. The only movement of significant amounts of Gold was from the mines to the temples or, occasionally, to the furthest reaches of the empire as a pacifying tribute.

Crossing the Line

This latter movement had great pertinence to the unfolding story of money. It established the situation whereby Gold was handed over in return for something received. These pacifying tributes were the first time that Gold was used for exchange—Gold for security/peace. Without any preconceived idea of the momentous ramifications, the line between the old world and the new was being crossed.

The Tomb Robbers

The English Egyptologist, Nicholas Reeves, produced an authoritative study of tomb robbing with the conclusion that the primary targets were Gold and silver. At first, the Gold that was released by the tomb robbers was in small amounts. It was not until circa 1500 BC that tomb robbing became widespread and the amounts stolen more substantial.

By 1100 BC, most of the tombs had been looted. The temple police could not outwit the ingenuity of the determined thieves, many of whom were the same people who had built the tombs. The desecration was vile; the wilful destruction of the beautiful Gold artefacts heart breaking, but the result changed life on Earth for the better. Maybe there was also a natural justice in the forceful destruction of that which had been accumulated by force.

Ultimately, in this whimsically peculiar universe, only ideas survive. Even the grandiosity and might of the pyramids themselves could not have withstood the eternal ravages of the millennia. The thieves only hastened the inevitable.

The increase in tomb robbing and the simultaneous increase in the flow of Gold from Nubia were unlikely to have been a coincidence. The emergence of Gold in the marketplace saw the rise of a new and vital dynamic to human existence. Gold had jumped the divide from the spiritual to the temporal. People wanted Gold to trade with.

There was almost certainly another factor in the emergence of Gold subsequent to the mining in Nubia. This was the practice in all places and all times of Gold being skimmed off by those working and running the mines and by those charged with the supervision of its transportation back to the treasury.

It can be reasonably speculated that it was both the increasing activities of the tomb robbers and the 'unofficial' Gold from the Nubian mines that loosed the dazzling Genie of Gold from the lamp. Whatever the means, Gold was no longer the exclusive property of the Pharaohs. It became money throughout Egypt, and from there, the known world. Despite the efforts of despots throughout the ages, the Gold Genie has remained on the loose.

The more that Gold began to find its way into the hands of the general populace, and the more that its wondrous properties desired by everyone became demonstrated, the more Gold emerged.

The First Golden Age

During the reign of the female Pharaoh Hatshepsut (beginning circa 1479 BC and lasting for 22 years), trade with the empire expanded dramatically and unprecedentedly. By the time Akhenaten came to the throne circa 1379 BC, Egypt had reached the zenith of her wealth and power. Most of the artefacts and architecture that are associated with the magnificence of Egypt came from this period of the New Kingdom, including the great temples of Karnak and Luxor and the Valley of the Kings. Drama, literature, art and music flourished and reached levels of realism that were markedly different from prior periods.

Egypt became incredibly rich. It has been assumed and stated that this was because of the increase in the flow of Gold after the takeover of the Nubian Gold mines. This is superficially correct. That there was a connection between the Nubian Gold and Egypt's sudden prosperity is true, but it requires a closer inspection to unveil precisely what that connection was. Up to that point, Gold had not transitioned to the marketplace—it had no commercial value. It had been hidden away behind lock and key and heavily armed temple guards.

Gold in hoards cannot increase trade. It was the emergence of Gold into the marketplace, Gold in circulation, which saw Egypt become rich. Like blood in the human body, it is circulating money that brings life to commerce.

For thousands of years, intelligent use of the Nile had ensured that Egypt was famous for its abundance. The New Kingdom achieved a level of prosperity that far surpassed all that had come before. Something major happened in Egypt circa 1500 BC, and that 'something' has never been satisfactorily explained. It was the exit of Gold (and silver) from the hoards that led to the zenith of Egyptian wealth and influence.

The Egyptian New Kingdom was the world's first Golden age.

The emergence of Gold into the marketplace heralded the beginnings of a prosperity that spread beyond just the ruling class. Circa 1500 BC is when humanity entered the modern world.

There is no evidence of Gold in general circulation prior to this point. The theory that Gold gradually, over a vast number of years, assumed dominance as the most useful method of exchanging goods, the most marketable good, is wrong. There was nothing gradual about it. When Gold exited the Pharaonic hoards and began to circulate, it took off like a horse from the starting gate. It ran fast and far.

The Phoenicians emerged from impoverished fishing villages on the coastal areas of the Levant to become a legendary maritime trading force. The Minoan traders from Crete reached their peak soon after 1,500 BC. The Greeks rose to such prominence that their fame has never faded. Within a few hundred years the economy of the whole eastern end of the Mediterranean was transformed.

With the ability to easily and precisely exchange surplus goods, society took a huge leap forward. It evolved into a more egalitarian model of existence that allowed for a measure of independence from the state. No longer would a nation's accumulated wealth be solely in the domain of the ruling class with the people reduced to toiling for handouts. They still held the majority, but Gold's blessings had broken their bounds. Public acceptance of the institutionalised poverty of a centrally planned economy was forever undermined. Gold in circulation, in the hands of the people, had unleashed the genius of the free market.

The circulation of Gold beginning around 1500 BC was the 'big bang' of social evolution.

The First Coins

Although its spiritual connection was still very much alive, Gold had broadened its sphere of relevance. The limitations of barter, and the cumbersome uncertainty of trade goods were forgotten as exchanges became easier, faster and more precise. Yet there was still an impediment to the full expression of Gold. It was over 800 years before the next innovation took place.

Circa 650 BC, the first coins were minted[**] in Lydia (what is now western Turkey); they were coined from electrum, a mixture of Gold and silver and called 'staters'[***]. They were flattened balls rather than coins. It is not possible to date them exactly as no dates were stamped on the early coins. The dates given vary depending on the source—always subject to archaeological interpretation. Doubt has been raised as to whether these first coins were created for the marketplace, or whether they were some type of religious token. No matter their origins; the people knew a good thing when they saw it.

It was not until some point soon after 560 BC, again in Lydia, that the first Gold coins of a set weight called 'Croesids' were introduced. The coins represented history's first easily recognisable known weight and fineness of Gold. As noted by Herodotus, Lydia became the location of the world's first permanently situated retail shops[****].

King Croesus of Lydia is credited with having these first Gold coins minted. That is more plausible than the unsubstantiated claim that it was one of the prior kings, either Alyattes or Sadyattes, who had minted the original staters. Coinage came to the attention of royalty only after its success in facilitating trade. What would those who relied wholly on plunder for their wealth know about the working of the marketplace?

Croesus became the first ruler to assume a monopoly of the right to coin money.

[**]   There is mention of an earlier coin—a Gold Shekel circa 1500 BC. No such coin existed. Alexander Del Mar *History of Monetary Systems* suggests that coins in a decimal division were in use hundreds of years earlier in India, but the source for this is obscure.

[***]   To be precise 'one-third staters' (trites). No full stater has ever been found and it would seem reasonable to just call them staters.

[****]   Herodotus famously referred to the Lydians as a nation of shopkeepers.

The Persian king Cyrus, whose army overran Lydia, adopted the practise of minting Gold and silver coins and also the practise of claiming the sole right to do so. The subsequent journey of coinage throughout the world was accompanied by the idea that it was the ruler who had the right to this lucrative monopoly.

As in the old world Gold had been monopolised by rulers for its spiritual properties, so in the new world it was re-monopolised for its temporal properties.

———❦———

Today, some people assume that Gold is no longer money because it is not used for commercial transactions. That belief overlooks money's primary role as a store of stable value. Central Banks have always known that Gold is money. Why else would they keep so much of it stored away in vaults behind metre thick steel doors? Why else would Gold be assigned an international currency code—XAU [*****]? Why else would Gold trade on the currency desks of every major bank and brokerage firm? They have all known that Gold is the one and only money, they just could not understand why.

They have not been alone.

———❦———

Gold existed for thousands of years alongside barter, but without either function or presence in the marketplace. It was only after Gold emerged from the temples and tombs that barter and trade goods became consigned to history. When Gold did enter the marketplace, it swept all prior crude attempts at exchange aside. The world was changed forever.

To gain a better understanding of the miracle of Gold circulation in the modern world (post 1500 BC), the following are its most important requirements. Not only is Gold the only store of stable value, it satisfies almost all the practical requirements of the marketplace.

[*****]   ISO 4217 Currency Code List

The Requirements of Money

1. *A high value compared to weight and volume*—One ounce of Gold will fit into a teaspoon. A very high value of Gold can be carried in a person's pocket. Money must be of an appropriate size for both transacting and hoarding.

2. *A useful value in the everyday marketplace*—In its traditional coin form, Gold has not been able to satisfy this requirement as its value has been too high.

3. *Fungible*—Fungible means that any sample is the same, and therefore as acceptable, as any other sample. Coffee and wheat come in all sorts of different grades, so are not fungible. One ounce of fine Gold is as acceptable as any other.

4. *Divisible*—Gold is very easy to divide and to reform

5. *Durable*—Anything that can be broken or burnt or that can rot or rust or otherwise deteriorate is unsuitable as money. Gold is almost indestructible

6. *Mouldable*—Money has to be soft enough that it can be moulded and stamped with a weight, but not so soft that the shape becomes distorted or easily worn.

7. *Recognizable*—Gold is recognizable by its unique colour. Silver too has a unique look. Even children used to handling the monetary metals can tell whether a Gold or silver coin is real or not.

   'There is not a child who does not know how to estimate the metal of the ingots and its degree of purity.'
   Father de las Cortes (missionary) 1626

8. *Transferable*—Money can transfer a value, not just from hand-to-hand, but also from one side of the planet to the other. Money is easily transferable and is accepted wherever people trade. Money is a store of stable value not just over time, but also space.

9.   *Permanent Agreement*—The French paper money of the late
     18th century had Madame Guillotine to enforce its status as
     legal tender. It was still rejected by the people. The agreement
     that something can act as a replacement for money cannot be
     lastingly imposed by force of law. People from all over the world
     chose Gold as money.

It is the singular quality of a store of stable value that gave humanity its one
and only money. The extensions of this quality were then given application
in the marketplace where they brought about an abundance of surplus
goods and wealth. It was money that facilitated the ultimate expression of
humanity's productive genius.

But can this be shown more conclusively, or will it remain just a
plausible theory? Does an understanding of the alignment of the Sun God
with Gold in a monetary sense, as opposed to just an archaeological one,
gain in credibility by leading to further clarity on the subject of money?

Chapter Six
Value

The value of a principle is the number of things
it will explain.

Ralph Waldo Emerson

A closer look at the mechanics of precisely what it is that Gold is doing in the marketplace is not only warranted, it is 3,500 years overdue. The errors have been so long-standing and so profound that the real story of money, both what it is and what it does, has to be painstakingly built from scratch.

Taking the theory that money is defined as a store of stable value and coupling that with the certainty that goods are 'of value', then value is a connection that is central to every transaction.

Can an exploration of value lead to a deeper understanding of money?

Whether value is objective or subjective has been twisted into philosophically complicated knots that require untangling. It is beyond sensible debate that some things, such as air, water and nutrition, have objective value to the human existence. Importantly though, a short contemplation puts it also beyond debate that the individual assessment of the *quantity* of value is always subjective.

Like the value placed on goods, this assessment will change from person to person and from moment to moment. A drowning person will place a high value on air and a low value on water. A value can be objective, but the amount of value is always subject to the evaluation of the individual. A body, lacking the determination of the individual as in the situation of a full coma, has no scale of values; it just has requirements, without which it will cease to function.

It is the individual determination of the *quantity* of value, subjective value, which is the key to the story of goods in the marketplace.

The Value of Goods

Each individual is in a constant state of value assessment.

When someone arises from their seat to go to the next room it is because they value being in that room more highly than staying in their seat. If someone makes a cup of tea it is because they value making a cup of tea more than doing something else with their time—at that point. The values change constantly; no one makes and drinks tea all day long—apart from authors suffering from writer's block.

The marketplace is no different; perceptions of value are not stable.

The value of a raincoat is high when it is raining, but probably moves to a lower value when the sun comes out; in the desert it could go to zero value because of its weight and be thrown away. The value of a bag of apples tends to be low if one already has a full fruit bowl at home or a laden apple tree. A person who places a high value on peanut butter sandwiches will place zero value on them upon being diagnosed as gluten or nut intolerant. Buggy whips were a hot item in the 19th century, but demand cooled off considerably in the 20th century.

All goods in marketplaces everywhere are subject to changes in individual perceptions of value.

What is a Good?

The attempts to define a good have been almost as unsatisfactory as those for money. A good is generally described in economics as being something produced in response to what is needed and wanted—something that has economic usefulness. While true, this description is superficial; it lacks the precision and depth necessary to provide any real insight. A more thorough inspection of the concept of value should also lead to a clearer understanding of goods.

Whether a particular value is objective or subjective can be left to one side. There are two other categories of value with far more importance to an understanding of what is happening in the marketplace. They are:

a. Exchangeable Value such as goods (hereafter referred to as goods value), and

b. Non-Exchangeable Value, such as aspirations, desires and aesthetic pleasure (hereafter referred to as core value).

Though seemingly connected in only the most tenuous manner, these two categories of value are inextricably linked and shine a spotlight on what a good really is.

All goods in any marketplace anywhere are produced in the attempt to give form to a core value—to turn a non-exchangeable value into an exchangeable value.

It is the core value of being warm and dry (non-exchangeable) that led to the making of clothes and shelters (exchangeable); the core value of wanting to be safe that led to armour and air-bags; the core value of wanting to look pretty that led to lipstick and manicures and the core value of a love of music that led to CDs and music teachers.

All goods without exception, including services (intangible goods), can be categorised in this manner. A good is properly described as an exchangeable, quantifiable value produced in the attempt to interpret and meet the requirements of a non-exchangeable, unquantifiable value. This is the precise meaning behind 'satisfying the needs and wants of the marketplace'. The goods value manifestation of a core value cannot represent the original core value in its entirety; otherwise it would be the core value. This fuller and more precise understanding of value neatly produces the answer to 'what is a good?'

A good is defined: 'An exchangeable, quantifiable value'.

Core values are intangible. They span the whole sphere of human existence. Each person possesses his or her range of core values. The perception of aesthetic value attached to the sight of the dew on the morning rose will probably remain with a person for a lifetime; as will the value placed on family, integrity, friendship, loyalty, truth, honour, love, beauty and pancakes. The range of core values also covers such things as gardening, exercise, theatre, sport, literature, hunting and art. The list is endless. Core values tend toward stability.

It is different with goods values; these tend toward instability. Not being the original core value, but a material manifestation of some part of that value, they do not inspire the same stability of allegiance. The core value of being warm and dry will likely remain stable, but an overcoat will not; it will either wear out or become unfashionable. The tech buff's 'must have' gadget of today, for which almost any price will be paid, is the obsolete technology of little perceived value in three years time. Some other gadget will have taken its place.

The core value tends toward stability; the goods value, its marketplace derivation, tends toward instability, but only relative to the core value that inspired it. The value of a 1967 Kalamazoo Gibson semi-acoustic guitar will always be dependent on the core value that inspired its purchase—a love of guitars or beautiful musical instruments, whatever. But that goods value guitar could well have a more stable value than the core value of a love of fluffy bed dolls.

The premise is not that all core values are necessarily more stable than all goods values, though they tend to be, but that all core values are more stable than their immediate goods value derivatives. Core values are not necessarily positive; an irrational hatred of a particular race of people is a core value in the same manner as a love of butterflies.

Of no consequence to the story, but of interest, is that the material advance of a society consists of giving ever-more sophisticated form and substance to core values.

Degrees of Stability of Value

Are some core values and some goods values more stable than others? The unambiguous answer is yes. The core value of being free from hunger is likely to be more stable than the core value of a love of hip-hop. The goods value of a jacket bought for its comfort and style is likely to be more stable than the goods value of a yo-yo bought on a whim. Values, both core and goods, can be classified in terms of their relative stability, though the precise order of that stability depends upon the perceptions of each individual.

So we have one type of value (core value) that tends to more stability than another type of value (goods value). We also have further degrees of stability within each of those two categories. The point of all this is the discovery of a shifting scale of stability of values.

A scale by definition is a graduated range, which means that it has end points—extremes. Logic insists that at one extreme there must exist a value that is the least stable and, at the opposite extreme, a value that is the most stable. The least stable value is purely theoretical, as being a good it will be constantly changing. Heading toward the other end of the scale are the more stable core values. At this extreme exists one particular value that is constantly the most stable.

The Exception

All core values on the scale are non-exchangeable and intangible—with just one, solitary exception. The core value of being 'at one with god', or however one wishes to phrase it, had an exchangeable form—Gold. Though this value was formed in the distant past, its monetary significance makes that value even more relevant today. It was this complete and stable core value, the original and whole value in exchangeable form, and the stock-to-flow ratio that it led to, which presented humanity with an intensely powerful gift—money.

The value that exists at the opposite end of the value stability scale from goods is Gold.

Goods are an unstable, quantifiable value; money is a stable, quantified value. Gold is a core value in exchangeable form. That Gold is a store of stable value has been observable in practise over thousands of years; it is now validated by theory. None of this should be construed as meaning that money is the most important value. It simply means that it is the most stable value.

Relative Stability of Values	
Gold Value—quantified and exchangable	Stable
Core value—unquantifiable and non-exchangable	Tends to stability
Goods value—quantifiable and exchangable	Tends to instability

CHAPTER SEVEN
THE SIMPLICITY OF MONEY

Money, industry, and goods reciprocally produce each other,
and float along in busy circles.

Novarlis

When Gold transitioned into a store of stable value, it became a money-in-waiting. The match made in heaven was consummated when Gold first entered the marketplace circa 1500 BC as a trading super lubricant. The emergence of money was an historic event unparalleled in importance, either before or since. It is inconceivable that an event of such magnitude in human history will ever happen again. All future progress, no matter how startling, will stem entirely from the discovery of the marketplace applications of Gold. The discovery of the wheel pales into insignificance by comparison.

> Money is perhaps the mightiest engine to which man can lend an intelligent guidance.

Alexander Del Mar *History of Monetary Systems.*

Money's remarkable attributes transported us from subsistence living to the age of the Internet. It also produced an enduring mystery—what is money?

The Definition of Money

The reason that the study of money and thus economics has become an area of such divergent and conflicting opinions is because at no point along the way did students begin the process by precisely defining the terms. Only when the definitions exist, are in accord with observable reality and logic, and are known and understood, can meaningful studies begin.

Gold only became money when it began to circulate in the marketplace. Gold is a store of stable value, but it has another defining characteristic when it circulates as money. The original theory that money can be defined as a store of stable value turns out to be wrong, close but no cigar. Money cannot simply be defined as Gold.

Fortunately the error was so slight that the theory did not run off the rails before it was discovered. The definition of money, though obviously correct, has remained unrecognised to this point. Because Gold is the only store of stable value and therefore the only measure of value, money must be defined:

A known weight and fineness of Gold.

There is no more to it than that. Ah, but what clarity can be gained from such an exquisite simplicity.

———⦿———

The Two Roles of Money

The understanding of Gold, together with high precision definitions for both goods and money, provide a crystal clear insight into the two unique roles that money performs in an exchange. They are:

1.   To measure value
2.   To be a known value

Both of these roles are devolved from, and remain dependent upon, a store of stable value. In all applications of money, one or both of these roles can be seen in action.

To Measure Value

The fact that goods have no inbuilt value, just a perception of value, has caused money's role as the measure of value to be, at best, expressed in somewhat vague terms, and at worst, totally denied; e.g. 'Money cannot be used to measure the value of goods because goods have no intrinsic value.' Though seductive, this logic is wrong. People do not use money to measure the value of goods for it is true that goods have no measurable value. What is happening is that they are using money to quantify their own perception of the value of a good at any particular moment. It is only with this understanding that the vital role of the measure of value can be appreciated.

Science is in a constant search to find more and more stable measures. A measure is that thing which is most stable; nothing in the physical universe is stable in an absolute sense. It is the speed of light that now defines a metre and atomic clocks that define a second. The kilogram is still measured by the original kilogram bar in Paris—'Le Grand K'.

All measures, whether of time, distance, weight or volume etc., exist because they are the most stable amongst a number of candidates. Each is under constant threat of abandonment as more precise (more stable) ways of measuring are discovered. Gold is under no such pressure. As the only occupant at the furthest point of the spectrum of stability of value, it is peerless. As the only measure of an amount of perceived value, money is the closest to an absolute. All measures must, by definition, be free from the taint of individual perception.

Money has objective value. No more precise measure of commercial value will ever be obtained.

To Be a Known Value

The two roles of money are manifest in all transactions and in the order enumerated. In the first role (the measure of value), the potential buyer and seller of the good each use money to quantify their own perceptions of the value that they place on the good. An exchange will only take place when these evaluations are in accord—when a price is agreed. This is when the second role of money (to be a known value) manifests. The good is exchanged for an objective representation of the value subjectively arrived at—money; a known weight and fineness of Gold.

At the point of transaction, this second role of money is so closely aligned with the first that it hardly seems necessary to make the distinction. The second role has another function though, one of the utmost importance and which has no immediate bearing on transactions. This will be looked at later in the book. But before that, money's role as the measure of value needs to be inspected in more detail, for this provides further, much needed, clarification on the nature of its relationship with goods.

Chapter Eight
The Measure and the Measured

And God created the two precious metals, gold and silver,
to serve as the measure of value of all commodities. They
are also generally used by men as a store or treasure. For
although other goods are sometimes stored it is only with
the intention of acquiring gold or silver. For other goods are
subject to the fluctuations of the market, from which they
(gold and silver) are immune.
Ibn Khaldun, Al Muquaddimah (circa 1379)

The irreplaceability of money's stability of value has sailed over the heads of modern economists. Ibn Khaldun's matter-of-fact 14th century wisdom would produce blank faces today. When it has been noticed, its importance has been largely ignored.

Is money a science that has always been misunderstood, or has it been a lost science? Ibn Khaldun hints at the latter, though there is little supporting evidence.

The vital nature of stability of value is made clear by a close look at the process that precedes an exchange. Had the logic not inexorably led to this point, then the real story of money could have begun here, for this is where the role of Gold and the definition of money move beyond what is supposed to what is demonstrated. The initially somewhat implausible origins of money demonstrate their validity. Following logic from a falsity cannot lead to simplicity and truth.

For a good to change hands in exchange for money, both parties must have gone through the process of subjectively measuring the value that they each place on the good. Only when this process is complete and when the results are in accord can the transaction occur. The decisive first step is the quantification of perceived value by both participants. If the seller measures the value of the good at 1.1 grain of Gold, and the buyer measures the value of the good at 1 grain of Gold, then no transaction will happen; the values are not in accord. Not a single transaction can take place until this measurement process has run its course.

This process should be instantly recognisable to anyone who has ever bought or sold any good in any culture anywhere.

An example would be the situation where someone sees a shirt in a store window with a price ticket on it. The person likes the shirt and would like to own it. He or she looks at the price and decides whether or not they value the shirt that much. If they do they buy it, if they don't they don't buy it. The process is not complicated. Both parties measure the value. The hopeful seller has measured his or her value and placed it on the price ticket; the potential buyer will either agree or disagree with that measurement. An agreement is a sale; a disagreement is no sale. The value is measured by both parties—always.

No transaction can happen in the absence of something to measure the value. The blindingly obvious nature of what is happening has somehow avoided scrutiny. How could a person know how much money to hand over for a good, or how much to accept for a good, if the coin was not able to accurately measure his or her perception of the good's value?

A Gold coin would have no meaning in the marketplace were it not the measure of value.

In the instance of a direct barter this process of measurement takes the form of: 'is his bike worth my cell phone, and, with the other party, 'is his cell phone worth my bike? One party is using the cell phone to measure the value of the bike, and the other party is using the bike to measure the value of the cell phone. In a barter situation these are the most stable values available and hence the most precise measures.

If money is in circulation then even in a situation of barter they will still use the monetary measure as guidance. If the bike is judged to be worth ten grams and the cell phone about the same then they will probably do the deal.

The three constants in every single transaction, whether using money or barter, are:

1.   Two or more parties

2.   A good or goods

3.   Something exchangeable that each party can use to measure their own perception of the value of the good or goods

As only the most stable value can be the ultimate measure of value, then the most stable value is entirely, obviously and undeniably the prime requisite for money. Money is only useful in the marketplace because of its ability to precisely measure and exchange value. Lacking either of these qualities it would not be able to perform the role of money.

The economist Carl Menger gave as his most fundamental axiom:

... value does not exist outside the consciousness of men.
Principles of Economics—Chapter III The Theory of Value

Simply translated this means that people have their own perceptions of value in the marketplace. What is very valuable to one may be of low value to another. Similarly, what is of a certain value to a person one moment is of a changed value at another.

This is true.

Menger however then went on to dismiss the importance of stability of value and the measure of value.

> 'But it appears to me to be just as certain that the functions of being a 'measure of value' and a 'store of value' must not be attributed to money as such, since these functions are of a merely accidental nature and are not an essential part of the concept of money'

Principles of Economics—Chapter VIII: The Theory of Money

This is not true.

Menger inexplicably chose to not follow through with his own logic. If value exists only in the consciousness, then the consciousness has to be in a process of evaluation—measurement. Either this, or the quantification of value at the level of the individual is random—subject to no rationale. It can only be the one or the other. If a measure of value is indeed mandatory to the process, which it is, because it is evident that the process is not random, then the fact that the measure can only exist in the presence of a stable value becomes of supreme importance.

To state that money can be anything other than a store of stable value is to state that the process of valuing goods and transacting is illogical and dominated by arbitrary whim. For this to be true, money and goods would have to be given away and acquired without rhyme or reason.

It obviously is not true.

Menger made many original and valid observations on the nature of the marketplace and money and it is not the intent of this book to denigrate a fine body of work, which has been of immense benefit to students. It has to be stated though that he also committed to paper the egregious howler that money evolved over thousands of years; that through a process of natural selection Gold assumed dominance as the preferred trade good.

The emergence of Gold's stability of value into the marketplace gave it instantaneous status as money. At the very point of discovery, Menger turned his back on his own logic and thus the true definition of money.

> Humans are the measure of all things.
>
> Protagoras (c.490—c.420 BC)

———∞∞∞———

Is Gold a Good?

It depends.

Without a correct understanding of Gold, money or goods, confusion has reigned supreme. Only once each is understood can a clear insight into the relationship between them be arrived at. The measure cannot also be the measured. Gold in monetary form is the measure of the perception of the value of goods; ipso facto money is not a good—academic protestations notwithstanding. Goods are subject to constantly changing perceptions of value. Money stands stable and aloof from this process.

Gold can still act as a good. A Gold bracelet is not money; the weight can be probably ascertained without too much trouble, but the Gold purity cannot. The bracelet is not 'a known weight and fineness of Gold'. This lack of 'a known value' means that the bracelet has not attained the status of money. If the bracelet was stamped with a credible .99 and there were scales available, then it would be money. Money does not have to be shaped like a coin—it just has to be a known weight and fineness of Gold.

If there were any value assigned to the bracelet above its weight however, then that would be the value of a good. If the bracelet contained 20 grams of .99 Gold, but an exquisite design or some other quality caused the assigned value to be 23 grams, then 3 grams would be the value placed on the design—or whatever feature it was that attracted the excess valuation. That part of the bracelet would be a good. The bracelet would be composed of 20 grams of money (stable value) and 3 grams of good (unstable value).

The fact that money is not a good is confirmed by supporting logic ...

The Diminishing Value of Goods

It is an understood and accepted principle in economics, as well as being readily available to personal experience and observation, that the more one has of a good, the less perception of value each additional one will have[*]. The second will be valued less than the first, and the third will be valued less than the second etc.

The classic example is the parched man in the desert. A water salesman approaches and offers him a bottle of water for two grams. Though it is an exorbitant sum he accepts. After that he is no longer parched and will no longer value the water as highly. He will probably buy another bottle, but only if the price is much lower. He may then decide that he would like another bottle to keep himself comfortable until he gets to the oasis, but that third bottle in turn has dropped in value considerably from the second.

A tech geek may save for a long time to buy the latest handheld device. No matter how much value he put on it and paid, the offer of another one would not attract the same perception of value. So it is with every good in all situations. At the level of the individual, they have a declining perception of usefulness.

That is not so with what is used to purchase the good—money.

At the moment that the good most desired is purchased, so another good moves into the category of 'most wanted'. The list from 'most wanted good' down to 'least wanted good' is in a state of flux, with new goods constantly entering somewhere on the list. There is always something occupying the 'most wanted' category. There is more to this than meets the eye though and it is necessary to delve deeper to appreciate the full mechanics of what is happening.

[*]   The theory of marginal utility—Carl Menger

Over and above this list of most wanted goods is a list of core values; the senior values that inspire the manufacture and purchase of the goods. Even someone in the unlikely situation of seemingly having all the goods that they want, still has their core values. One in particular, the core value of future security, is of immense importance to the story of money as will become clear later.

Money has no decline in marginal utility because the desire for the expression of core values is infinite.

It can be easily reasoned and observed that all goods decline in marginal utility[**]. This points us in the direction of a logic that is, if all goods decline in marginal utility and money has no such decline, then it is incorrect to think of money as a good.

> All goods decline in marginal utility
> Money has no decline in marginal utility
> Money is not a good

The theory that the less a good declines in marginal utility, then the closer it approaches being money, is in serious error. There is no such thing as 'degrees of moneyness'. Something either is money, like a known weight and fineness of Gold, or it is not, like everything else. A good cannot be money. A good with a slower than normal declining marginal utility can though be a useful trade good. The theory of marginal utility, while useful to an understanding of the exchange of goods in a barter economy, has no bearing on the subject of money.

———— ⬥⬥⬥ ————

Paper money[***] does have a declining marginal utility. Those who prosper

[**]   The clearest explanation of this is in *Beyond Mises* by Rudy Fritsch

[***]   It should be clear by now that the term 'paper money' is an erroneous concept; paper cannot be money. It will be used in the book nevertheless because of its familiarity. At some point in the future, the term is likely to be used as a pejorative meaning something that was once thought valuable but which turned out to have no value whatsoever. As in a paper money employee, a paper money job or a paper money contract.

under the system of paper money splash it out to gain ever less valuable goods and services. The more paper they possess, the less value it has. Paper money is not accumulated in the same manner as real money. Hideous mansions and garish yachts and accessories are the natural end phenomena of this declining marginal utility. The tacky lifestyles of 'the rich and famous' in the 20th and early 21st centuries are legendary. This fall in the marginal utility of paper money explains the noticeable fall in the quality of many goods over the last century.

This should not be confused with technological advancement. The technology in houses and cars and most other goods is vastly superior to that of one hundred years ago—there is no end to human ingenuity. At the same time the quality of the construction has generally diminished. The imperative is to consume paper money, not to preserve it. An overall decline in the quality of goods is the logical consequence.

Paper money chases goods; goods chase Gold.

This is the consumption promoted by those 20th century economists responsible for luring governments into the current disaster. A frenzy to consume, to the neglect of accumulating (hoarding or saving), is the leading indicator of a terminal decline in the perception of paper money as a store of stable value. Paper is a good, whether it has numbers printed on it or not. Therefore it should come as no surprise that it has a declining marginal utility. Paper money has no stability of value and therefore cannot perform either of money's roles over the long term.

> Gold is the monetary metal par excellence because it has constant marginal utility.
>
> Professor Antal E. Fekete
> *The Gold Demonetization Hoax*

———⟨∞⟩———

No matter the angle of the approach, it is quite clear that money is not a good. It is not that Gold is 'exempt' from the equations of supply and demand as has been claimed. It is that these equations can only apply to goods; they do not and cannot apply to money. How could money be the measure of the value of goods in the marketplace, if money itself is a good subject to perceptions of value? The failure to grasp this elementary truth has added another level of complicated error to money.

The confusion that has caused money to be spoken about as a good has resulted in endless academic discussion as to whether Gold is a present or a future good. Gold of an unknown weight and fineness is a present good. Gold in the form of money is not a good at all, but can be exchanged for a good, either in the present or the future.

Gold in any form is a store of stable value. Until it is has achieved a known weight and fineness, we just don't know how much value. Only once it has achieved this can it enter the marketplace as money and perform its two roles.

As one of these roles is as the measure of value, it is impossible for it to be also the value measured.

———— ✦ ————

A close inspection of exactly what it is that money is doing in every single transaction gives instant access to the certainty of what money is. That the precise nature of money's true functions has been so overlooked by so many economists over so many centuries means that the study of economics has to return to step one.

To arrive at a better understanding of money, it is necessary to deconstruct the errors of the old understanding. Even the little that has been known about money has been at the least, distorted, and at the worst, twisted beyond all recognition. The erroneous lumping together of money and goods has led to a significant misunderstanding that has further degraded the subject area.

The remorseless tug of the unfolding logic demands that this be dismantled before the story of money can progress any further.

CHAPTER NINE
THE GRAND UNIFIED THEORY

Before I came here I was confused about the subject.
Having listened to your lecture I am still confused,
but on a higher level.

Enrico Fermi

The beginnings of the use of trade goods are forever lost in the mists of unquantifiable time. The Tin Road from Afghanistan to Mesopotamia circa 2700 BC and, soon after, the Silk Road from China to Ancient Egypt, provide the first credible records of international trade. Egyptian mummies from this period have been found wrapped in Chinese silk. There are strong hints that the Egyptians and Indians were trading far and wide for thousands of years before this.

Intrepid traders with their caravans of tin, silk, spices, medicines, slaves, ivory, precious stones, perfumes, furs and sundry other trade goods snaked across the plains and through the valleys of the world. International commerce began long before the dawn of money. Trade goods were not as effective as money, but humanity's irresistible urge to produce and exchange was not to be entirely thwarted.

It was these traders, risking all in the eternal quest for profitable exchange, who linked up the dispersed cultures of the world.

Bear in mind that both parties in a volitional transaction regard it as a profitable exchange. When a volitional exchange happens, it does so because both parties believe that they will profit from it—gain an advantage from it. Not an advantage over the other party, but an advantage over their own prior situation.

It is worth noting as an aside, that along with the goods travelled new ideas. While these ideas were not quantifiable, their ramifications were often even more beneficial to the recipient societies than the goods. The traders, who are negligently absent from our history books, were of far more importance to the development of our world than the mighty warrior heroes with their deeds of slaughter, town-gutting and culture destruction.

They still are.

> To plunder, to slaughter, to steal, these things they misname empire; and where they make a wilderness, they call it peace.
>
> Tacitus

Academia Strikes

The term 'medium of exchange' seems to have been first used in the early 18th century*, though it did not enter common usage in economic texts until the 20th century. In the late 19th century the similarly mysterious and daunting 'most marketable good' arrived on the monetary scene. Both these dense terms are superfluous to an understanding of money. Reduced to their essence, they mean the same thing—'trade good'. There is no more significance to them than that. A medium of exchange is any trade good. The most marketable good is the best trade good. They have no bearing on the story of money, despite prolonged and muddled efforts to show otherwise.

---

* Massachusetts 1714—despite extensive searching, no earlier mention was found, though that does not mean it does not exist.

For millennia, trade goods were called as such. Their sudden and clumsy transition to a medium of exchange and then a marketable good, mark the precise points where money, which previously had been a simple subject, became very complicated. The experts from academia moved in as swiftly as common sense and logic packed their bags and moved out. Money was made unutterably complicated and then declared to be a science. It is nothing of the sort.

The terms became widespread as a result of the intellectual contortions necessitated by the attempt to slot paper money into the category of money (medium of exchange) and money into the category of a trade good (most marketable good). It was the effort to form a Grand Unified Theory. There is no possibility of a theory that unifies these differently evolved phenomena.

The acceptance of this error has been as complete as the confusion that it has wreaked. The tenacious exploration and promotion of the Grand Unified Theory has created a tangled mess. The more painstakingly the subject has been explored, the further it has wandered from reality and the more complicated and contentious it became. That is because there is no such subject; there is no valid theory that unifies these disparate entities.

Money was not an evolutionary process that led to the most marketable good—always a tentative and fragile theory. Gold had been hoarded for thousands of years and already had a large stock-to-flow ratio before it emerged into the marketplace. Money is not a science, money is just money—a known weight and fineness of a store of stable value.

Once this is understood, all the confusion falls away. When money circulates freely then no monetary scientists are required because everyone can naturally and easily understand the essential features of money.

A Good For a Good

Prior to the emergence of money, a trade good was often accepted in exchange for a good, even though it was not the good specifically wanted. This occurred only because of a reasonable level of confidence that the trade good could be exchanged for the good that was really wanted later. Such things as cows, goats salt, dried fish and seeds were all used as trade goods at some place and point in history.

Every single trade is a good for a good—either in the present, or the future. This is the only connection between money, barter and trade goods. The connection is genuine, but it is an error to attempt to use this as the foundation for a theory of further similarity. Comparison ends at the point of stability of value. Money sits serenely at the most stable end of the value spectrum; goods, including trade goods, erratically prance around at the most unstable end. Money could never have emerged from such a fury of infinitely convulsing value variables.

In the absence of money, a trade good acts as the best available store of value until the person finds the good that they really want, or until they can exchange it for money. Sometimes, as in barter, both parties receive the good that they want immediately. More often, one party receives the good that they want in the present, and the other party receives a trade good that they can exchange for the good that they really want in the future. This explanation provides us with the definition:

> Trade good: 'an easily exchangeable good used to transfer value into the future.'

Prior to the emergence of money, trade goods were very useful. The requirements of trade goods were that they:

    a.   were perceived to hold their value more stably than most goods,

    b.   were in demand,

    c.   had a useful value in the marketplace, and

    d.   were easily transportable when necessary.

Trade goods were a natural and useful innovation that arose from within the marketplace. They had far more application than direct barter, but lacked the guaranteed stability of value of money.

—∞∞∞—

Why Money is Superior to Barter

With direct barter, both parties receive what they want simultaneously. Without question, the direct barter of a good for a good is not only the simplest; it is the most efficient form of exchange. While being without peer in its efficiency however, it is almost barren in its applicability.

The difficulty with a successful barter is that it must display a coincidence of both wants and values. Each party must want what the other is offering and the goods must be mutually measured as being of comparable value. A coincidence of wants and values is so unusual as to place an enormous impediment in the way of the exchange of goods. Money makes the improbable trade entirely possible. Trade goods show their worth in a similar, but far less effective way.

It is not for nothing that the time of direct barter is referred to as the Stone Age.

—∞∞∞—

While all goods were subject to fluctuating demand and valuation, some tended to hold a demand and value more stably than others. It was these that were the best trade goods. The cigarettes used to facilitate exchanges in WW2 prisoner-of-war camps were sometimes referred to as money. They were not, but they were the best available trade good. They were selected because they were the most stable, in demand and useful value available to the prisoners and were easily transported (and hidden).

The millennia of barter and trade goods were not times of widespread prosperity. While trade goods were a great improvement on the direct exchange of barter, they were a far cry from the sophistication of money.

Goats were a valued trade good, but it was not always convenient, or even possible, to tow along a herd of goats looking for the good that was really wanted. Trades were still hard to make. Retail shops did not, could not, exist and even markets were few and far between.

The reality is that a 'medium of exchange' and the 'most marketable good' are just convoluted terms for plain old trade goods. In the interests of untangling a chronic confusion (three hundred years), trade goods are receiving a whole chapter here. The reality is that they are worth little more than a small footnote in the lustrous story of money.

———— ❧ ————

Commercial Transactions

Paper money is usually described as 'token money'—a representation of money. As it embodies none of the properties of money, is not redeemable for money and is no longer even thought of as a representation of money, this is clearly a misnomer. As token monies are goods, albeit of the most inconsequential kind, it provides some sort of clarity to think of them as token trade goods. They are typically of no or very little value, but are accepted because of the belief that they will be exchangeable for value in the future. Unlike a real trade good, their miniscule value means that they are reliant upon trust.

There is no real exchange with these tokens, because the paper is not of sufficient value; ipso facto they are credit instruments. Paper money is accepted because of the belief that 'promise to pay', or 'full faith and credit', means that it will be exchangeable for a good at some future point. Tokens work until the trust that underpins them is lost, or, put another way, the credit providing entity defaults.

There are four ways of commercially transacting. They are in order of the most workable over time:

1. Money
2. Trade goods—indirect exchange

3. Barter—direct exchange

4. Paper money—no exchange

———∞———

What money does in the marketplace is not solely what money is. First, foremost, indispensably and by definition, Gold is a store of stable value. It is the extensions of this quality that are used in the exchange of goods. There are a few ways of exchanging goods, but there is only one store of stable value. Money's highly visible role in the exchange of goods has resulted in the assumption that anything that does a similar job must be a type of money.

This assumption exists in every book and school of economics, and in every dictionary. It has been solidly locked into the realm of conventional wisdom. Like much else in the study of money, it has been just as solidly wrong.

Two Separate Developments

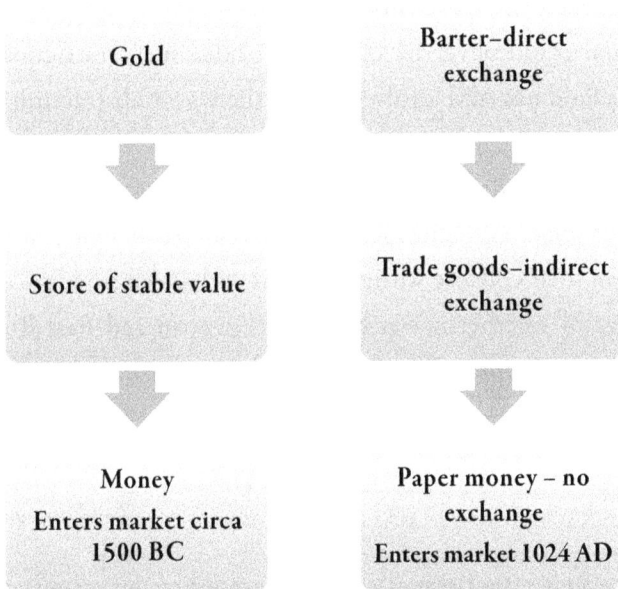

Gold	Barter–direct exchange
⬇	⬇
Store of stable value	Trade goods–indirect exchange
⬇	⬇
Money Enters market circa 1500 BC	**Paper money – no exchange** Enters market 1024 AD

———∞———

Paper is not a store of stable value and for that reason it cannot properly perform either of the roles of money. It can though be made to circulate in the short-term because:

   a.   it is in genuine and widespread demand (within national boundaries) because of the legal requirement that government taxes must be paid in it, and debts can be paid in it,

   b.   it has a useful apparent value because numbers can be printed on it representing a wide variety of units,

   c.   it is easily transportable and, for as long as point 'a' above exists, easily exchangeable, and

   d.   Transactions involving Gold and silver are rendered impractical by government taxes—capital gains among others.

The tribes of Central and South American and pre-New Kingdom Egyptians (among others) proved that large groupings of people could exist with barter and trade goods alone. A society, with freedom instead of serfdom, could never have evolved under such restrictions. They certainly could not have evolved under the wooly abstraction of paper money.

Only after the development of Gold's marketplace application was it possible for societies to emerge. Of more than passing interest is that all these began their collapse when Gold was withdrawn from the equation, irrespective of whether it was by theft (Egyptian and East Roman) or government bankruptcy (West Roman, British and American)[**].

> A great civilization is not conquered from without until it has destroyed itself from within.
>
> Will Durant

[**]   The collapse of the Harappa/Mohenjo Daro society may be the exception. While the society was built on Gold, there is no available evidence that points to the collapse having a monetary cause.

Money is far superior to trade goods, which have a stability of value only relative to other goods. Money stably stores value for all time and everywhere and is in constant demand. Even in the theoretical extreme of a complete absence of surplus goods, Gold will continue to hold its stable value, not only in anticipation of their re-emergence, but as the incentive for them to do so.

It was money that created the modern world. Money in circulation blows wind into society's sails. Today our societies sit becalmed. Worse, the weight of paper debt is causing them to sink. Money and trade goods are two separate marketplace phenomena. A trade good is a crude way of exchanging goods; its only virtue is that it is less crude than direct barter. A trade good and token trade goods are what is used when there is no money. Carl Menger's theory that money originated from the most marketable good is a confusion of two separate developments.

The unstable value of trade goods proved a major stumbling block to the advancement of human tribes, and not only because of difficulties at the point of exchange. It is here that the story returns to the second role of money: 'to be a known value'.

CHAPTER TEN
MONEY'S PRIMARY FUNCTION

*Money is a guarantee that we may have what we want in the
future. Though we need nothing at the moment it insures the
possibility of satisfying a new desire when it arises.*

Aristotle

The accumulation of money presents a very negative concept in the western
world. It is associated with greed for the sake of greed and disparaging jokes
about 'saving up to die'. Scrooge McDuck[*], who made his first appearance in
1947, as part of Disney's long running *Donald Duck* cartoon, is the epitome
of the public's view of accumulators. A bespectacled cartoon character
wearing a top hat and a monocle, he spent his days either diving into or
counting his Gold coins.

Scrooge was labelled a miser. The depth of this pejorative can be
understood by its etymology—'miser' is from the Latin meaning 'wretched'.

Two generations grew up with this portrayal of accumulators fixed in
their minds. Following the grim years of the US depression, Uncle Scrooge
came to symbolise more than just a figure of fun, he came to represent
much of the resentment that had built up in people; people who still had no
idea what or who had caused the terrible poverty of their parents' lives and

---

[*]   Named after the similarly maligned Ebenezer Scrooge from the Charles Dickens'
classic: *A Christmas Carol*.

their own childhoods. It not so subtly permeated the public consciousness that accumulators were despicably greedy people who meanly grasped Gold to their bosoms, while others starved.

It was a grossly misleading portrayal of something of incalculable virtue.

Money Makes Money?

Once Gold began to circulate in the marketplace as money, some of it began to be transferred back into hoards. In the course of time this meant that many of the hoards of a stable value accumulated over thousands of years became transformed into hoards of a known value. The difference in potential was profound. As a statement, 'Money makes money' is incomplete; it is more correctly stated: 'Accumulation of money makes money'.

It was in these accumulations that 'to be a known value' demonstrated its real importance to the story of money. Trade goods did not lend themselves to being accumulated. A herd of goats or cows was subject to disease and aging; grains could rot or become infested. Long-term accumulation of wealth using goods, which by their nature are of an unstable value, involved considerable uncertainty—risk. It is the unique ability of money to be a known (and stable) value that motivated its accumulation.

Many items can be used to successfully exchange with, as the long history of trade goods clearly shows. While exchanges do not have to involve money, the storage of a stable value over the span of time does. This stable value storage, which can only be performed by Gold, has far more relevance to the story of money than the transfer of value that can be performed by any number of trade goods.

It is only by its accumulation that the complex benefits of money become wholly unveiled. A society will flourish in direct proportion to individual and business accumulations of money. This is the feature of money that changed the course of history. Accumulations mean investments. Investments create new technologies, products and jobs and thus even more opportunities to exchange. The ease and speed of trade brought about by circulating money is very visible. It is the far more discreet (and almost uninspected) accumulations that ensure this smooth exchange of goods is in a continuous process of moving to higher and higher levels—an infinitely rising spiral of material advancement and general prosperity.

The entry pass to this prosperity spiral is the willingness and ability to produce goods that are needed and wanted and acceptably priced. With that in place, even the humblest can accumulate wealth, and with that they cease to be humble.

Only the freedom to produce and accumulate surplus wealth has the power to break down the world's archaic and artificial social divisions between those born to privilege and those born to poverty—between those whose children will always go to Eton or Harvard and those whose children will be condemned to grind their way through a government supplied, bog-standard education.

It is accumulations of money that ensure the marketplace is a vibrant organism. Circulation of money facilitates trade; accumulations of money expand trade. The circulation of money was paramount to the trade that saw the beginnings of societies, but the ability to store a known value was paramount to societies' growth.

Money shines most obviously in the exchange of goods; but it shines most brightly in its accumulation.

———∞———

The Power of the Future

Though all exchanges are of the essential nature of a good for a good, this is far from the totality of the process. More important to building a sophisticated economy is that surplus goods can be exchanged for future security. That security, in the form of accumulations of money, is still representative of goods for goods, but it is the security that is paramount, not any specific good. This exchange of a surplus good for future security is the real driver of economic progress.

The desire for survival into the future is a core value common to all sane people; its satisfaction in the present is a goods value. It is worth repeating that a core value has more stability than its good's value derivatives.

The promise of the future good has a far more profound influence on general and sustainable prosperity than the fact of the present good.

It has been claimed that a better understanding of an economy can be gained by removing money from the equation** . This on the basis that exchanges are always of the nature of a product for a product and money only detracts from an easy understanding of the operation. This is false. Studying an economy on the basis that it is always just an exchange of a good for a good in the present overlooks the stupendous importance of surplus goods being exchanged for future security.

It is the certainty of future goods, a certainty that only money can guarantee, which is paramount. The specific nature of those future goods is irrelevant. It is the idea that whatever they are they will be obtainable that is all-important. That is what security of future means. So important is this that people will do without goods that are wanted and even needed in the present in order to obtain security of future.

The person who 'does well' has sacrificed present goods in order to obtain future security via accumulation. These accumulations are the foundations upon which, not only personal wealth, but also a thriving and expanding economy are built. The social gain from the aggregate exchange of goods is profound, but immense potency is created by the far-reaching gains that derive from accumulations.

**   French economist Jean-Baptiste Say (1767—1832)

Money performs a much more important role than that displayed in the momentary function of the exchange of goods. This is another of the major errors that has caused economics to founder. Money is more than just a tool of the present; money is the fullest expression of future possibility. Using paper monies that cannot transmit a stable value through time severely degrades the prospect of future survival.

Only Gold can carry a stable value through time; thus it is Gold that gives the best assurance of future. Lacking the ability to carry value into the future, people can only subsist in the present. The withdrawal of Gold from circulation will eventually bring about a reversion to subsistence living.

The tendency to hoard is one of the most virtuous traits of humanity. Accumulation displays foresight; the ability to not only predict, but to act in accordance with that prediction. It also aligns with the basic imperative of economics, which is to create reserves. Accumulations, in the form of both hoards and savings, are simply reserves—manifestations of surplus production and prudence.

Hoarding was the earliest form of personal insurance and remains its simplest demonstration to this day. Many things can facilitate an exchange in the present; only Gold can provide the stable value that will guarantee the validity of that exchange into the future.

Gold savings with interest are not currently possible because money is not circulating. Paper money is not saved because interest rates are too low to offset the constant degradation in its value. Without either Gold or paper savings, investments and jobs will continue to disappear. The vertical spiral of prosperity created by Gold will degrade and reverse under paper money to become a downward spiral into ever-deeper poverty.

That process is already well under way.

The best tool for future security (after reason) is money. Accumulations of money are material manifestations of reason.

It is apparent that the enhancement of survival by hoarding and saving does not just benefit the individual. They are the bedrock of a complex economy. Commercial activity begins with accumulation, which leads to investments, then production and jobs and which create a surplus, exchange and prosperity. The cycle repeats ad infinitum ...

The Money Cycle

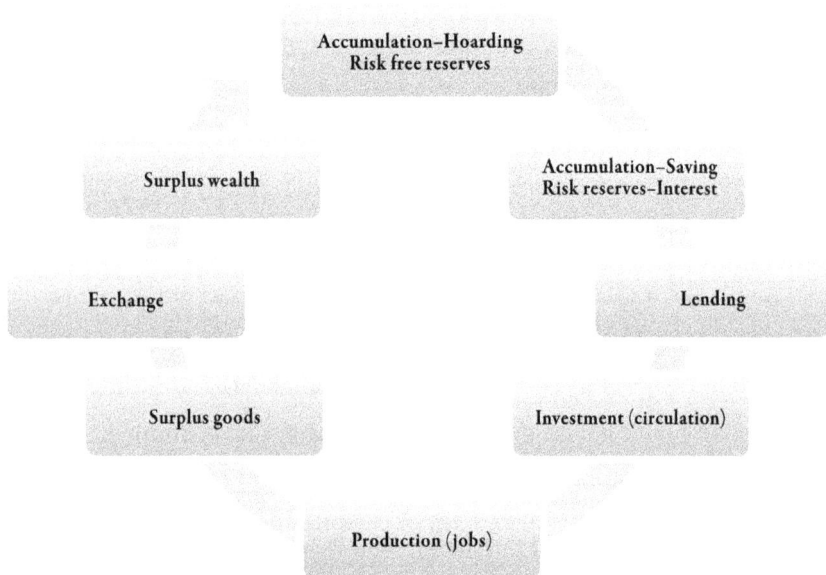

Accumulation–Hoarding
Risk free reserves

Surplus wealth

Accumulation–Saving
Risk reserves–Interest

Exchange

Lending

Surplus goods

Investment (circulation)

Production (jobs)

The production of surplus goods creates prosperity at the point where they are exchanged. Prosperity cannot be created without exchange. To view the commercial world solely at this point of transaction though is to observe just the last part of a long and sophisticated process; yet this is where the focus has been. The exchange is the final dab on the masterpiece. Neither this nor the preceding brush strokes could exist to any great degree were they not laid on the foundation canvas of the ability to accumulate a known and stable value.

It is in the nature of the human existence that the present is a temporal vantage point, from which a rational person concentrates on decisions affecting the future, no matter if the future is a millisecond away, or many years distant. With the study of money and economics, the present has been examined without reference to, or awareness of, the predicted future circumstances that bring about these present actions.

It is the predictions of the future that command the present and author the past.

In every volitional exchange, each entity would consider that they were creating a better future for themselves because of the exchange; otherwise they would not proceed. A person exchanges their labour for a wage because of the belief that they will be better able to support their family with it than without it. The person who pays the wage does so because they anticipate a gain from doing so. A person exchanges money for groceries because of the family meal due that evening. A car is serviced so that it will not break down.

When extrapolated out across billions of commercial interactions, it is the vector for future security that explains the story of the production of surpluses, the story of human achievement and advancement and the story of the rise of societies. The myopic focus on what good is being swapped for how much money—the present 'what', is of far less consequence than the future 'why'. The production and exchange of surplus goods, the basis of prosperity, will not happen to any great degree absent a store of stable value.

———— ◦◦◦ ————

Profit and Value Storage

The overriding story of the history of the exchange of surplus goods has been the pursuit of stability of value in order to ensure future security. Surplus production has little merit if its value cannot be stored.

Profit itself is secondary to value storage.

Why would people suffer the risk, time, cost and effort of producing surplus goods without the means of storing the wealth that they represent? Why bother? This is why prior to the circulation of money, certain goods evolved as trade goods; their primary value was not the goods themselves; it was the perception of their relative stability of value. When absolute stability of value was discovered in the form of Gold, the world moved onto a different plane of existence.

It is the individual urge for future security that has driven humanity from sheltering under trees and in caves to the high-tech and comfortable age of the 21st century. In the absence of the store of stable value, this thrust of humanity for future security cannot be satisfied.

———∞———

Money's first and foremost function is, and always has been, as a means of storing and accumulating value. This is its primary role that cannot be performed by anything else. It is from this that money's stature, desirability and increasing stock-to-flow ratio derive.

Money's use in the exchange of goods is a secondary function.

This must not be construed as in any way diminishing the importance of this role. Though the accumulating dog wags the tail of exchange, and money is replaceable in the exchange of goods, the nature and extent of exchange would be severely degraded without it. No trade good could ever adequately replace the measure of value. The point is that exchanges could and would still happen without money; accumulation of a stable and known value could not.

———∞———

Scrooge Sanctified

The wholesale withdrawal of money from circulation and into hoards in the early part of the 20th century resulted in the loss to common perception of the store of stable value. The damage has been incalculable in the form of widespread malinvestments and a series of booms and busts. Those who still understood intuitively that Gold was a store of stable value were too few to make a difference.

It is the growing number of Scrooge McDucks, those who accumulate real money from their surplus production rather than investing in trade goods or frivolously consuming everything, who will lead this world out of its deep malaise. These people are the Praetorian Guard of society. At some point in the not too distant future, Gold will come out of the hoards to again bless the world by circulating in the marketplace and being available for the creation of sound investments and real jobs.

No one would save in the knowledge that what was being set aside was reducing in value. Only a store of stable value over time, or what is perceived to be one, will be accumulated. For this reason, once suspicion is aroused, paper money is neither hoarded nor saved; it is spent. It is this necessity, this urgency, to pass on paper money for something of more stable value that leads to investment 'booms'.

Chapter Eleven
Booms, Bubbles and Busts

Gold is forever. It is beautiful, useful, and never wears out. Small wonder that gold has been prized over all else, in all ages, as a store of value that will survive the travails of life and the ravages of time.

James Blakely

Booms, bubbles and busts have captured the popular imagination for centuries. With the passage of sufficient time, the sense of tragedy is replaced by bewilderment that humans could have acted so gullibly.

Then it happens again.

How easy it is to identify and observe the peculiarities of an earlier age, and how difficult it is to study one's own age with the same clinical detachment. Yet, though there have been numerous suggested explanations for these speculative frenzies, including 'the madness of crowds' and 'too much money in circulation', the real reason has not been touched upon.

These destructive episodes relate to the story of money only inasmuch as they are restricted to periods when money is absent—either because of adulteration, or the circulation of paper money. The store of stable value is so crucial to existence that in its absence, an alternative has to be located.

Life provides each producing person with three monetary options:
1. Live for the moment with nothing surplus
2. Save
3. Invest

The vast majority of people prefer option '2'. Not many are so irresponsible that they fail to consider their own future security and that of their family, but neither do they have the time or inclination to become investors. They save their money in a bank and the bank invests it for them and pays interest. Not only are their savings holding a stable value, the amount is increasing. In this manner their old age, children's education and unforeseen eventualities can be faced with equanimity.

This option is removed with paper money. Central bankers constantly depreciate paper money. It is their stated policy to reduce its value by around 2% a year; the depreciation is often much more. Saving a paper money at an interest rate of less than 1% in the knowledge that it is falling in value by at least 2% is not sensible. To store wealth in the certain knowledge that it will diminish in value defeats the purpose of saving.

—ೞೞ—

When the attempt is made to have paper perform the job of money, the reverse occurs. Instead of measuring value in the marketplace, the paper is so volatile that it becomes measured by the value of goods. Paper money is the measured, not the measure.

> So how do we establish the value of Fiat ... ? Through the concept of 'purchasing power' ... that is, the value of Fiat is determined by what it can be traded for ... a so-called 'basket of goods'. But this clearly implies that Fiat has no value of its own, rather value flows from the value of the goods and services it may be traded for.
>
> Rudy Fritsch

The Relative Stability of Values Spectrum turns out to have a level of instability even lower than goods value—paper money value.

Today, the absence of the store of stable value means that saving is no longer a viable option. In consequence, the strategy has disappeared from public consciousness. People might occasionally still save in the short term for a specific purchase such as a holiday, but saving long-term, for future security, is no longer spoken, written or even thought about. Generations of people using Gold as money in the 19th century saved and achieved a security of existence that was unprecedented. With a paper money that falls in value and bank interest rates that fail to compensate, the only option remaining for the prudent person is to move to option '3' and become an investor.

The absence of circulating money and thus savings has meant that the world has become divided into those who live for the moment, and investors. The safe, conservative and traditional middle ground is not ignored; it no longer exists. It was savings that defined the middleclass, not because they saved, but because they could not rise to that comfortable level without savings. The amounts set aside each week by working people were small steps toward an accumulation sufficient to ensure future security.

Without savings there is no mechanism for a person to rise out of the drudgery of a week-by-week existence—other than investments. Lacking the skills and wherewithal required for investing, most resort to its bastard offspring—speculation: the purchase of an asset in the hope that it will rise in price.

—❧—

Along with encouraging borrowing, low and falling interest discourages savings. Isn't that perverse, to discourage saving? What happens when an entire society doesn't save?

Keith Weiner

But how can they become speculators when they have not been allowed to save any money to speculate with? All they have is the small surplus from their income. The answer is that interest rates are lowered even further and 'easy loans' become the order of the day. Bank loans are made available for speculation, particularly in real estate; instead of people saving the weekly surplus, they use it to pay off the loan.

Because almost all speculators are in the same situation, and subject to the same rumours and media prognostications, the moves in and out of various assets, such as real estate, stocks and works of art are immense and, for a time, self-fulfilling. It is a huge tide of paper money that ebbs and flows creating market distortions wherever the waves land and then, inevitably eventually, retreat.

As asset prices rise, people become exuberant. Governments quickly convince themselves that this is all due to their own brilliant stewardship of the economy. Based on this wisdom, they borrow even more (sell more bonds); new policies are announced and new handouts promised. The paper money begins to lose more value.

The government announces a new era of permanent prosperity.

The falling value of the paper money is inversely proportional to the rising price of the assets. There is a failure to understand that the goods are measuring the falling value of the paper; as it falls it takes more paper to buy the same goods. The speculators believe that the paper is measuring the asset value and that the assets are rising.

The government calls a snap election to humbly offer the people more of the same genius. They are re-elected with an increased majority.

The bell tolling the end of prosperity is mistaken for the starting whistle.

The Cause

Not all booms are malinvestments. The computer boom of the late 20th century was due to a genuinely large and rising demand, as was the early stage of the railway boom in the 19th century.

Unsustainable booms are a different matter; they are nothing more than manifestations of the market desire, the necessity, to locate a substitute for money's guaranteed stability of value.

In these false booms, real estate and selected other assets serve the purpose of trade goods. Without access to the security of money, they are perceived as being the most stable value available. They also give the prospect of appreciating sufficient to offset the falling value of the paper. This is acknowledged with inducements such as 'buy for the long-term' and 'bricks and mortar will always hold their value over time'. Note they do not say 'will always hold their price over time', for they know that this is never enough with paper money.

Real estate agents have intuitively understood what economists have overlooked; the single-minded drive of people always and everywhere for a store of stable value.

In the 20th and 21st centuries, salted fish and herds of goats have been replaced with real estate and works of art. In all instances they are third-rate substitutes for accumulations in Gold. It is not that Gold is not available; it is that it is not available to public perception.

The rise in demand for the selected assets leads to a rise in price. Eventually the process begins to snowball. More would-be savers start to believe that they are missing out on an opportunity and also enter the market. They are encouraged to borrow and chase prices even higher. This is where what begins as the healthy market pursuit of a substitute for stability of value moves into a destructive boom phase. The problem of the absence of the stable value is now compounded by the absence of the measure of value. No one knows the real value of anything.

Confusion as to the process in motion is rampant.

The boom is seen as a sign of prosperity and easy profits, instead of the harbinger of doom that it is. The consequent bust is a disaster, especially for those who are lured in at the final stages. What begins as the urge to locate a stable value in which to store surplus wealth ends up being the cause of massive instability of value in the very assets favoured.

The lack of money in circulation leads to the futile attempt to locate and accumulate stability of value by other means.

The government blames the bust on greedy speculators.

> *With the exception only of the period of the gold standard, practically all governments in history have used their exclusive power to issue money to defraud and plunder the people.*

Friedrich von Hayek—1974
Winner of the Nobel Memorial Prize in Economic Sciences

———⊶⊷———

The cheap bank credit and easy loans are usually cited as the cause of these booms and busts. They certainly facilitate and exacerbate the booms, but are not the cause. The real cause, the only cause, of these voyages into fantasy is the absence of money; it creates two insurmountable problems. First, stability of value has to be sought in goods, and second, there is no measure to properly assess the value of these goods—any goods, not just real estate.

It is money that acts as the warning bell all the way through the process. Money is always available to measure value were it to be consulted. It is humanity's misfortune to be living through the tail end of a period when its pronouncements have been ignored. The absence of the measure of value in commercial transactions is like the absence of instruments and stars to the navigator. That at some point the speculation will end on the rocks is certain.

Were value measured by money, these speculations could be seen for what they are far earlier. Were value stored in money, they would not happen in the first place.

———⊶⊷———

Bubbles

The eternal hunt for stability of value is the first step in that extreme of a boom known as a bubble. Theory insists that the first bubble would have been created sometime soon after 1024AD with the advent of the first paper money in China. The first record of such a bubble however and probably the most famous is the Dutch tulip bubble—also known as 'Tulip Mania'.

The tulip bubble had its origins in the Netherlands circa 1590, as a fad for the wealthy. The unusually vibrant colours and exotic origins (Ottoman Empire) of the tulips made it the status symbol of the time. In 1620 the steady price rises, which had been due to normal market demand, began to shift into something else—a manic, speculative investment phase.

The discovery that money is defined as a known weight and fineness of Gold, and that its absence causes booms, dictates that there must have been a lack of money in circulation for the Dutch tulip bubble to happen. A search of the records confirmed this.

The boom that became a bubble occurred because of the Europe wide debasement of coin during the 'Thirty Year War' (1618—1648). The debasement was severe. From 1619 to 1622, European nations minted counterfeit, low-grade coins of other nations. They then covertly sent them over the borders in an effort to hurt these other nations economically. They simultaneously and equally covertly debased their own coins in order to pay for the war—without apparently noticing the irony.

The war and adulteration caused the bankruptcy of most of the great powers of Europe[*].

---

[*]   It was only the audacity of the legendary Admiral Piet Heyn that saved the Dutch themselves from the international poor house. In 1628 he became the only Privateer to ever capture a complete Spanish treasure fleet consisting of forty-six tonnes of silver and an unknown quantity of Gold and goods.

Coins became so adulterated that children used them as playthings. It was so extensive that it is claimed economies as far afield as Britain and Russia were affected. The new Dutch Republic was famous at this time as the principal trading hub for the world. It became flooded with these coins from all over Europe.

With circulating coins of such dubious authenticity, how was wealth to be accumulated? No coin was above suspicion. The lack of an easily accessible known weight and fineness of Gold gave little choice to the Dutch but to chase stability of value wherever they could best find it. Tulip bulbs, which were initially a rational investment due to the long-standing and rising demand from the gentry and wealthy business people, seemed like a solution.

In the absence of money, only trade goods remain.

The high prices paid for the tulip bulbs of yesteryear are no different from the Alpine peak prices paid for 'investment properties', stocks and works of art at the beginning of the 21st century. What ended up as bubbles had the same cause—the eternal hunt for stability of value. It is not mania (madness) that precipitates that urge; it is future security (sanity)—though poorly executed. The validity of the original impulse is not negated by the fact that, in the absence of a store of stable value, the urge to store wealth can end up producing an extreme of irrational behaviour. The sole focus on the final step of the cycle, on the price at the point of transaction is where the mistake has been made. In a bubble, the exchange, the denouement of the process, comes many steps after the absence of the store of stable value begins it.

Studies have mostly concentrated on the attempt to plot the prices paid for the tulip bulbs, not the reason they were bought. The marketplace will always seek stability of value as its number one priority; it dominates every step of the Money Cycle, beginning with accumulation and moving through to the act of exchange and then, most importantly, back to accumulation representing the consideration of the future. In this manner the cycle repeats.

The last part of any bubble process is the peak of euphoria. Those who had sought to accumulate in a stable value, suddenly and inadvertently find themselves further round the Money Cycle producing a profit—heady stuff. It is at this point that the process gets out of hand (and crowded) and what was originally just the normal impulse for stable value eats itself.

There is a saying in real estate that reduces that subject to its simplest and most important feature ... 'location, location, location'.

Money can be reduced to the same level of simplicity: 'stable value, stable value, stable value'.

The real source of booms, bubbles and busts is confirmed elsewhere in history. Another famous example was the rampant clipping and counterfeiting of the English coin that brought about the stock market boom of the late 17th century. It concluded in the South Sea Bubble of the early 18th century. The constant shortage of coin in Scotland led to the use of debased English money. The result was the doomed Scottish adventure in Panama, the 'Darien Disaster', which is reported as consuming up to a third of the total wealth of Scotland. It concluded in 1707 with the loss of Scottish sovereignty. Yet another was the Mississippi Company Bubble that followed John Law's paper money experiment in France.

The price of monetary debasement has always been excruciatingly high.

John Law was one of the first economists to tub-thump the notion that money was merely a means to exchange goods. He did however still pay lip service to money's real nature. He backed his paper with land in the vain attempt to achieve some sort of stability of value. Needless to say it didn't work.

The market distortions brought about by the withdrawal of money from circulation and by legislating paper in its stead has inflicted more damage than can ever be assessed. It has tasked people and business with participating in a complex economy using a tool of exchange that would not have passed muster in a tribal village.

In the late 20th and early 21st centuries the situation has been exacerbated by the careful construction of almost insurmountable barriers to wealth creation. Businesses are confronted with byzantine regulatory hurdles; on top of which, governments have removed the only secure means of value storage, which greatly diminishes the virtue of making a profit anyway. Is it any wonder that the world's economies are collapsing? The real wonder is that at the time of writing people are not already starving in the streets.

The primary urge after immediate survival is to create a surplus of wealth in safe storage to ensure future security. Money is that safe storage. Gold did not become money because market participants thought that it would be a good idea, or because it is traditional that it be in this role. Gold became money because it is the only store of stable value that humanity has and for that reason and no other is the only money possible.

When safe storage is no longer available because Gold is no longer understood to be a store of stable value, then the urge toward future security degrades to the phenomenon of 'shop till you drop'.

This is the legendary 'fat lady singing' point that signals the imminence of terminal collapse.

In the early part of the 20th century, Gold retreated into hoards; replaced in the marketplace by government issued paper. Those paper monies have been on a one hundred year journey to the resting place of all their predecessors—curiosity shops, fireplaces and lavatories. That rendezvous with destiny is imminent. When booms bust and property values and stock markets collapse, most people are still young enough to recover. It is much harder for anyone to recover when what is used as money collapses. In the 21st century, the world is again on a desperate hunt for stability of value; it is hidden right under their noses. When they find it, the agreement that holds paper money in place will disintegrate.

Widespread and sustained misallocations will only happen with synthetic or adulterated monies, not real money. The world is, at the time of writing, still labouring along under the yoke of synthetic money, but what is paper 'money', why and how did it come into existence and why does it so reliably and regularly fail?

Paper Money

After almost one hundred years without money in circulation, it becomes of interest to relate the peculiar story of the attempt to synthesise money— paper money. The following is a stand-alone chapter that has no real bearing on the story of money and can be skipped or returned to later without any loss of momentum or sequence. It does serve the purpose though of explaining in more detail the mechanics of why paper money has such a dismal history.

Rudy Fritsch was my mentor when I began to study economics and money. It was with the greatest respect for his prodigious knowledge of paper money, coupled with his clarity of expression, that I asked him if he would contribute this section. He graciously accepted and, with some minor editing, this chapter is wholly his work.

This contribution to the book should in no way be taken as an endorsement of the ideas contained in it. Rudy has not even seen the other chapters, let alone endorsed them.

—⁂—

CHAPTER TWELVE
THE ORIGIN OF PAPER MONEY

*If you can't explain it to a six-year-old, you don't understand
it yourself.*

Albert Einstein

In order to best understand what money is, it helps to understand what money is not. Throughout history, many attempts have been made by governments to increase their power. These attempts are inevitably limited by constraints on the amount of money that they have at their disposal.

Since government does not produce value, its value is obtained through taxation. The amount of taxation that people will tolerate has limits and those who govern are generally aware that too high a taxation leads to unrest, potential revolution and even the collapse of an existing system.

The Romans tried to get around this limitation by adulterating their coins ... that is, by adding a certain amount of base metal to the money (mainly silver coins) in circulation. The idea was to increase the quantity of 'money' (number of coins) that the government controls (spends) by pretending that the adulterated coins were actually money. The market (people holding the coins) responded predictably; the purchasing power of the debased coins fell ... to the value of money (silver) still in the coins.

When first issued, around 65—68 BC, the Roman Denarius contained about 4.5 grams of silver. By 250 AD, it contained less than 0.4 grams. The decline of Roman money parallels the decline of the Roman state. Interestingly, the Eastern Roman empire, Byzantium, kept full value of its coinage ... the Bezant ... and Byzantium outlived the Western Roman Empire by more than a thousand years.

Clearly the confusion between money and government issued coins came early. A coin's value is the weight of Gold or silver it contains ... adding base metal allows more coins to be minted from the same quantity of monetary metal ... but at discounted value per coin. Once the quantity of monetary metal in a coin reaches zero, the value of the coin falls to the value of the base metal used to replace the monetary metal ... near zero.

—❦—

In the East

It was in China that the idea of using paper to replace Gold and silver originated. China had historically used silver money, but, like all other governments, they wanted more than they could tax. In 1024 AD, unable to acquire more silver, the Chinese emperors resorted to printing paper chits ... and using their military power to enforce the use of the essentially worthless chits as 'money'.

Once this process of using fraudulent paper as a substitute for money got going, the inevitable and seemingly never ending story ran its course; the value of the chits fell, in spite of everything the emperor could do. The holders of the chits, the common people, were impoverished. Impoverishment led to revolution, and revolution led to the fall of the dynasty. This process was repeated so often that in 1661[*] the Chinese finally passed a law making paper money illegal.

---

[*]   In a fascinating quirk of fate, in exactly the same year (1661) that the Chinese banned paper money, the Swedish Riksbank introduced it to the west. PB

We may conclude that in China, money was ruled by power ... at least for a while. The monopoly of military power enjoyed by the emperor allowed him to decree that his signature on a chit made the chit 'as good as money'. His power inevitably fell with the falling value of his chits ... and the very paper money he decreed to be the 'currency of the realm' led to his demise, and to the demise of his dynasty.

———⊶⊷———

In the West

In the Western world, things developed differently. When Marco Polo completed his epic voyage, he brought gifts from the Chinese emperor, including Chinese paper money. The idea of paper money was a total novelty for the West; when the King and the Pope saw the Chinese paper, they decided that this was a creation of the devil ... and burned it. Nevertheless, a few hundred years later the West was enslaved by the very same 'devilish creation'.

There was no European empire, thus no emperor with the power of monopoly to decree that his chit shall be money. Europe was divided into many small kingdoms; each King was powerless beyond his own borders. Nevertheless, all these Kings needed ... or wanted ... more money. Unable to create money at whim by simply printing it, they were obliged to borrow.

It turns out that in the West, money ruled power. The bankers had money, therefore power ... and the Kings were obliged to march to the bankers' tune. Thus Western paper money was not simply printed, it was borrowed into existence. The bankers got their pound of flesh in the form of interest.

The process whereby paper money came into existence in Europe is fascinating, and highly educational. Conventional wisdom holds that the genesis of paper money was 'fraudulent Goldsmith warehouse receipts'.

Supposedly people were reluctant to carry Gold and silver coins, and consigned their money to the Goldsmith, in return for a receipt. Then, the receipts were used as substitutes for actual coins ... i.e. the receipts were used to make payment.

It is assumed that the Goldsmith soon realised that all his receipts were never redeemed at the same time ... and he simply decided to print more receipts than he had Gold or silver on hand, and pocket the profit. This theory assumes that the Goldsmiths were fraudulent from the get go, and that the people living at that time were naïve enough to fall for such a cheap scam.

Interestingly there is no historical evidence supporting this scenario ... and plenty of evidence supporting another, far more realistic theory. This other theory is based on the history of Bills of Exchange that circulated (were used to make payment). It is important to the story to understand that these Bills of Exchange were in wide circulation hundreds of years before bank notes, or even banks, came into existence. In order to understand this theory, we first need to understand what a Bill of Exchange is, how these bills came into existence ... and how they evolved into bank notes.

The very name 'Bill' gives us a clue; when merchandise changes hands, a bill is presented, accepted, and paid. In a restaurant the bill is sometimes called a 'check' ... but the process is the same. Eat, receive bill, accept bill, pay bill. Simple.

The difference between a retail bill such as the restaurant check and a commercial bill is the term; rarely are commercial bills paid in cash on the spot. Most commercial transactions include terms of payment, such as 30 days, 60 days, or 90 days. In other words the merchandise is delivered, the bill is presented, and the bill is accepted. Payment will be made on maturity of the bill ... when the bill comes due. The date of maturity depends on the terms written on the bill itself.

The Circulation of Bills

The transition of a commercial bill to a Bill of Exchange came later ... and this transition was a natural advance in the economy, an advance created by the free market. In England the historical record shows very clearly that Bills of Exchange circulated; that is, they were used to make payment. Circulating Bills played a temporary, but vital monetary role. Temporary because once paid, bills are retired ... and vital because circulating bills increased the efficiency of Gold money most spectacularly.

For example, suppose the local pub receives a few kegs of beer; instead of paying cash, the proprietor signs the bill, agreeing to pay in full in 45 days. The brewer then has a signed (accepted) bill that will be paid from the proceeds of beer sales. The term granted gives time enough for all the beer to be consumed, so that the pub owner need not put up any cash ... but simply accumulate the monies paid by the beer consumers, and pay the bill when it comes due from this money.

The bill held by the brewer represents value; the value of beer in high demand by consumers ... consumers who will pay for the beer. Instead of simply holding the bill till maturity, the brewer may offer to pay his suppliers with this very same bill. This is the crux of the Bill of Exchange; it is a document that carries value in terms of consumer goods in high demand, goods already in existence, and is a document acceptable to other merchants as a means of payment.

The actual process of circulation is simple; the brewer will endorse the bill to his supplier, by signing it and writing the name of the new holder on the back of the bill. For example, 'I, Bob the brewer, hereby endorse this bill to Harry the hop supplier' ... and when the bill comes due, the pub owner will not pay the brewer, but the hop supplier ... or whomever the bill is endorsed to.

When the Bill is endorsed to another party, it is not traded at full face value, but at a discount. This is crucial; no one desires to pay full value for paper promising Gold in the future. Every time a Bill is endorsed to a new holder, the discount is re-calculated ... the market value of the bill is determined by the time remaining to maturity, and the current discount rate.

The acceptor of the Bill ... i.e. the pub owner ... has a commitment to pay the bill at face value at maturity ... this is given. However, if offered a discount, the pub owner may decide to pre-pay his bill; pay before the due date. The counterparty, the holder of the bill, has an incentive to get cash now ... and is generally prepared to give some discount for early payment. The interplay of these two forces, across the whole bills market, sets the market rate of discount.

Notice that the spending propensity of the consumer is the ultimate driver of this interaction. If the retailer i.e. pub owner has an abundance of paying customers, and thus plenty of cash in the till, he will likely agree to pre-pay the bill for a modest discount. Conversely, if business is slow, if consumer spending is trending down, the retailer will demand a steeper discount for prepayment.

Now, not all commercial bills qualify as Bills of Exchange. Only bills drawn against products in high demand will be accepted as payment ... a bill drawn against beer is clearly desirable and will easily circulate. It is not likely that the beer drinking public will suddenly decide to all become teetotallers. Similarly, a bill drawn against flour will circulate; people need to eat, and surely flour that is used to bake bread will sell.

A bill drawn against cloth is perhaps not quite as secure ... while people do need clothes, there is also a question of changing fashions ... and good reason that no Bill of Exchange has a maturity of more than 91 days ... a quarter of a year, a season. Cloth that may sell well enough in summer may not sell in fall ... or winter.

Furthermore, if push comes to shove, clothes can be mended and used longer; this is not true of beer or bread. Bills drawn against the most urgently needed goods will circulate more readily, more quickly, than bills drawn against less desirable goods.

A bill drawn against lumber or bricks, or specialty tools, will probably not circulate at all. If the product stays in inventory, money for paying the bill will not flow to the retailer. These kinds of bills remain simple commercial bills. The funds used to carry inventory for such products must come from elsewhere than the bill market; either from the merchant's own capital, or from borrowing. Notice that Bills of Exchange involve credit, credit granted by the suppliers, but not borrowing.

So, bills may circulate; some circulate particularly fast, others more slowly ... and some not at all. Those Bills nearest to Gold will inevitably circulate the fastest. And which Bills are nearest to Gold?

Bills of Exchange drawn against a Goldsmith, a Gold refinery, or a Gold mine will circulate most readily, and fastest; after all, the pub owner still has to sell the beer ... and the bakery the bread. On the other hand the Goldsmith, the refinery, and Gold mine actually hold Gold in inventory; they do not have to sell any merchandise to get Gold. Bills drawn against the Goldsmith, the refinery, or the Gold mine will circulate most readily, will circulate the fastest.

To sum up, some bills don't circulate ... they do not enter the bill market, the stream of Bills of Exchange ... or as Adam Smith called it the 'Social Circulating Capital'. Some bills will circulate ... and some bills will circulate very fast. To see what this means, understand that every time a Bill of Exchange is endorsed to a new holder, the back of the Bill needs to be signed; for example. 'This bill is hereby endorsed to Harry the hops merchant' by the previous holder, Bob the brewer.

If the bill changes hands often, the back of the bill is soon literally filled with endorsements, and a new bill for the same merchandise with the same value and maturity date but with a clean back must be written by the acceptor ... the pub owner. This is a hassle.

Furthermore, every time a Bill is endorsed to a new holder, the discount is re-calculated ... the market value of the bill is determined by the time remaining to maturity, and the current discount rate. For example if we have a Bill with a face value of one hundred Gold units and a time to maturity of 90 days that changes hands at a price of ninety nine units, then the discount is one Gold unit (annualized 4%).

If this bill changes hands in thirty days, the discount will now be 2/3 of a Gold unit. In another 30 days, the discount will be 1/3 ... and on maturity the discount disappears as the bill is paid in full ... at face value.

Holding this bill for thirty days gives a useful profit ... 1/3 of a Gold unit. If the bill is held only for a week, the profit is reduced to 0.083 Gold units (1/3 divided by 4); not very much. If the bill is held for a day, the profit on rediscounting (endorsing to a new holder) is further reduced, to 0.011 units. Now imagine that a particular bill is held only for a few hours before being spent; the trouble of re-calculating the discount is not worthwhile.

Because the Bill is circulating so fast, it becomes a nuisance to calculate the discount rate; it becomes not worth the trouble.

These factors drive the evolution of the bill; the acceptor (Goldsmith) decides to issue bearer bills instead of bills endorsed to a particular holder; no need to endorse the bill on it's changing hands ... whoever shows up with the bill at maturity will get paid. This is a big step in the evolution of the Bill of Exchange ... from an instrument that must be endorsed to each new holder, to a bearer instrument.

Furthermore, if the effort of calculating the discount is no longer worth the trouble, the bill will simply circulate at face value. If so, this implies that the maturity date has become irrelevant. After all, if the bill is not discounted but simply circulates, what difference does it make when it matures ... if ever? Value surrendered on acquiring the bill will be the same as value received on spending it ... there is no incentive or profit in holding this type of bill.

Finally, the merchandise the bill was drawn against also becomes irrelevant; since the acceptor has Gold on hand, what counts is the name (reputation) of the acceptor. It matters not if the merchandise the Goldsmith accepted is in demand or not; it is the position of the Goldsmith as a holder of Gold that counts.

If a Gold mine signs (accepts) a bill for dynamite, clearly the dynamite will never be re-sold to any consumers, but will be used up in the operation of the mine. As the bill will be paid out of Gold in inventory, this does not matter. There is no need for the mine to re-sell the dynamite.

Thus, all connection to the Bill market has been severed. The Bill of Exchange has morphed into a Note, redeemable in money (Gold or silver) by bearer ... at any time. A fully redeemable (freely exchangeable for Gold) bearer instrument with no maturity date, and no reference to any merchandise is clearly no longer a Bill of Exchange ... it is now a bank note ... a bank note has no maturity date, and is redeemable on demand. In this respect, a bank note is a more difficult instrument; redeemability implies that the Gold to redeem the bill must be on hand at all times, not just accumulated for payment on a future date.

One thing should be crystal clear; a bill, either retail or commercial, is NOT money ... indeed, it is the antithesis of money ... it is a claim against money to be paid right now (retail bill) or at a specified time in the future (commercial bill). A Bill of Exchange is not money, it is a claim against money to be paid in the future ... to whomever the bill was endorsed to.

Notice also, the US Dollar is called a Dollar 'bill' ... not a dollar 'receipt' or 'reci' as it would be if the Dollar really evolved from Goldsmith receipts.

What we use today as 'money' is not redeemable; it has not been for the better part of a century. We use IOU's as 'money' ... but IOU what? IOU nothing; only 'faith and credit' ... or more precisely, only the monopoly and military power of the Government. We have come, by a circuitous route, to repeat what the ancient Chinese did with their paper money.

The monopoly of military power enjoyed by our rulers today ensures that their chits are 'as good as money'. The rulers' power however still falls with the falling value of their chits ... the US Dollar has lost ninety-eight per cent of its value in the century since the US Bank of issue, the Fed, was inaugurated. The paper money decreed to be the 'currency of the realm' is leading to the demise of our current rulers, including the American dynasty. The ancient Chinese curse is in full effect; we indeed 'live in interesting times'.

This is where we are today; there is no Gold in the system, no extinguisher of debt ... and the consequent enormous tower of debt, now counted in trillions of Dollars, and in quadrillions of Yen, is consuming the world economy. The process of systemic destruction will not, cannot stop until real money ... Gold and silver ... are allowed to resume their historic roles.

Rudy Fritsch 2013

CHAPTER THIRTEEN
THE DISMAL SCIENCE

*Over the course of 600 years, five dynasties had
implemented paper money and all five made frequent use of
the printing press to solve problems. Economic catastrophe
and political chaos inevitably followed. Time and again
officials looked to paper money for instant liquidity and the
immediate transfer of wealth. But its ostensible virtue could
not withstand its tragic legacy: those who held it as a store
of value found that in time all they held were worthless
pieces of paper.*

Ralph T. Foster
Fiat Paper Money—The History and Evolution of our Currency

The modern world has been labouring under the delusion that the
occurrence of money was an entirely logical and obvious development.
Money has been thought of as an invention, with Gold chosen as just one
of the parts to make the invention work. The assumption is that the part
could be any of a number of options, maybe copper or platinum ... or paper.
Central bankers, the guardians of our paper money, are perplexed because
the latest version of the 'invention' is not working well.

The vital role played by stability of value has eluded them all.

They have assumed that what they saw money doing in the marketplace must be the entirety of its existence. This lack of focus on the past where stability of value was formed, and the future with its demand that stable value be accumulated, is the reason that the application of modern economic theories has failed so spectacularly. Economists have stared intently at the present and imagined that this was all there was to it. This approach has consigned the 'science' to not only failure, but also disrespect.

There is another school of thought that suggests the problem is even deeper ...

> 'The problem is, of course, that not only is economics bankrupt but it has always been nothing more than politics in disguise ... '
>
> Hazel Henderson

Whatever the cause of the intellectual disarray, it is not without reason that economics has been known as the dismal science.

It is impossible to overstate the importance of stability of value in any exchange beyond the direct barter of immediately consumed goods. Even with a trade good, the marketplace would reject one that was perceived to be diminishing in value. Why part with a valuable good if what is acquired for it begins to lose value—to become worth less than the good that you had?

The offer of a trade good would usually be accompanied by a sense of unease on the part of the person parting with the good. Would the goat being offered die or prove to have worms? Would the nuts go soft or mouldy? Would the value of copper collapse if a new mine were found nearby? Exchanges would still happen, but generally there would be no rush on the part of the owner of the goods to part with them. The incentive to produce surplus goods would be diminished.

In such transactions, the pressure is usually on the owner of the trade good to demonstrate that it is worth the good that he wants. When money is in use, the situation is reversed and the pressure will always, except in extremis[*], be on the seller to prove that the good is worth the money. This is the principal reason why prices will never be lower than when Gold is in circulation. Money demands the lowest possible price and gets it. Goods chase Gold.

The Limitless, Timeless Option

The possession of money is more useful than any single good because money can obtain an unlimited variety of goods, not just immediately, but forever. The exchange of a good for money is the exchange of a limited, short-term option for a limitless, timeless option. The desire for Gold causes an increase in both the quality and quantity of goods as vendors seek to gain an edge in order to obtain money.

This is why money freed up the markets in 1500 BC and why goods started to flow in far higher amounts than previously. The power of Gold as a store of stable value in the marketplace, is not only irreplaceable, it is irresistible.

This also makes clear why the criticism that 'one cannot eat Gold' is so senseless. When Gold is being used as money, there will always be a plentiful supply of goods. It is only when Gold is removed from the equation that shortages occur—including shortages of things to eat.

It is the quality of a store of stable value that underpins a thriving market. There is no effective substitute for this quality. Without money both circulating and accumulating, the world will return to the level of commercial activity of pre 1500 BC.

---

[*]   As in the example of the parched person buying water in the desert.

Goods do not measure the Stability of Money's Value

Instances of Gold buying more or less of a particular good have sometimes been misconstrued as meaning that the value of Gold has changed. The stability of Gold's value should not be taken to mean that the price of goods should always be stable as measured by Gold. In a world where demand for goods is changing, and where goods have no intrinsic value, only seven billion perceptions of value, there can be no stability of any good's price—either in the short or long term.

Nor is it desirable.

The value of each and every good is quantified at the point of exchange by individual perceptions of worth. These perceptions are changing—from person to person and from moment to moment. To try to achieve stability of prices is to attempt stability of perception—at best an exercise in futility, at worst the expression of totalitarianism.

The Roman Toga story is often pressed into use to prove the stability of Gold's value. The example is fallacious. It comes from the supposed fact that one ounce of money would buy a great toga in Roman times, and will still buy a great suit in the 21st century. When used to demonstrate the stability of money's value this is misleading. It is true that some goods can have a somewhat stable price over long periods, but this is the exception rather than the rule. We live in a world where the perceived value of goods changes. This will, and must for markets to operate efficiently, be reflected in their prices.

The toga quote is an example of the unusual stability of the price of men's clothing; it is not a legitimate comment on the stability of the value of money.

During the California Gold rush the price of wheelbarrows, picks and shovels increased enormously. From one week to the next, more and more money was required to buy them. This did not mean that the value of Gold was dropping; it meant that there was an actual, perceived or anticipated shortage of these necessary goods and the prices were bid higher accordingly.

Huge numbers of people were attracted to the Goldfields; 80,000 arrived in 1849 alone. The necessary implements were bid higher and higher because there were not enough for everyone ... until the free market supplied more at which point the price of wheelbarrows, picks and shovels etcetera moved straight back down again.

Talk of too much Gold causing prices to rise is poor research, tabloid economics—a superficial and sensational interpretation of events.

Between the prices of the wheelbarrows etc. rising and then falling again, the amount of Gold available from mining had increased. In that instance the prices dropped simultaneous with an increase in the amount of money available. When the goldfields were exhausted there was far more Gold above ground than when mining began, yet the value of wheelbarrows, picks and shovels was at rock bottom.

The quantity of Gold is irrelevant; it is the perception of value placed on goods that is always and everywhere the all and everything with price.

The same economics played out in the embryonic West Australian Goldfields a few years later[**]. As more and more people arrived in the outback to mine the plentiful Gold, so the price of water rose and rose. Then, as competition in the water supply business arrived, so the price of water plunged[***].

So it was with those who lived by selling their labour. The cost of a blacksmith at the Gold fields went up dramatically. That increase in labour charge was a normal market reaction for a service in high demand and short supply. As the Gold became mined out, so demand for the blacksmith fell—along with his price.

[**] It was no coincidence that Gold was found in Australia so soon after the Californian Gold discoveries. Gold had been noted as early as 1823 in Australia, but it had been deemed wise to suppress the news because of the mainly convict population. That changed when thousands of able-bodied Australians began to board ships heading for California.

[***] The underground water was almost entirely brine, which meant that crude but effective condensers were built. Julius M. Price *The Land of Gold*

The change in the price of labour and goods was, as always, entirely because of the change in the perception of their value.

—⊗⊗⊗—

Quantity and Quality Theories of Money

We must have a good definition of money,
For if we do not then what have we got,
But a Quantity Theory of no-one knows what,
And this would be almost too true to be funny.

Professor Kenneth Bouldings

The dispute that rages down at the bar every Saturday night as to whether it is the quantity or the quality of money that matters can come to an end. Well it doesn't really of course, but there is such a dispute in academic circles—honestly. It goes along the lines of: 'There is too much money being printed therefore the prices must rise.' To be countered by: 'No, it is not the quantity that matters, it is the perceived fall in the quality of the money that matters. When quality falls then prices rise.'

Like much else that has existed in the monetary science, it is based on a misunderstanding. The whole question is perched precariously on top of the confusion that money and paper money and goats and salted fish are all types of money and can all be evaluated in the same manner.

With money, because its fineness has been established, there can be no question as to its quality—.99. As to quantity, the more money there is, the more stable its value becomes as the stock-to-flow ratio demonstrates. Once it is understood that the only money is a known weight and fineness of Gold, then the debate becomes meaningless, which is why it has sat unresolved. Phrased as it is, it is unresolvable.

Both the quality and quantity of money are supremely important, but neither has any affect whatsoever on prices. The quantity/quality debate is one of the many unfortunate side effects of the Grand Unified Theory.

—⊗⊗⊗—

The spiritual origins of Gold have another surprising and important ramification that has straddled commerce from the time of the Pharaohs until the present. A complete understanding of Gold cannot be gained without an understanding of its relationship to silver. Each can only be fully understood in the context of the other. Gold and silver have a symbiotic and powerful relationship but, as with so many other aspects of money, much of that relationship has been misunderstood.

CHAPTER FOURTEEN
THE SILVER BULLET

Sail on silver girl, sail on by ... your time has come to shine,
all your dreams are on their way.

Paul Simon

Silver:

Chemical element symbol, Ag
Atomic number, 47

Ag is derived from the Latin word *argentum* meaning 'having the quality of shining'. 'Silver' comes from the Anglo-Saxon *Seolfor* or *siolfur* and refers to its colour.

Silver's association with excellence is not as prominent in the everyday language as Gold, but is still represented. A 'silver tongue' in the biblical sense* meant a tongue that belonged to someone who was just and upright in word and deed. It is more used today to mean someone who has a clever way with words.

A 'silver bullet' is an effective solution.

Sterling silver is composed of 92.5% silver alloyed with 7.5% base metal, usually copper. The copper gives the coins increased durability. In the same manner that the English language is replete with references to

---

* *Proverbs* 10:20 'The tongue of the just *is as* choice silver: the heart of the wicked *is* little worth.'

the worthy properties of Gold and silver, so specific reference is also made to the practical aspects of sterling silver ... as in doing 'a sterling job' and 'An if my word be sterling ... ' (Shakespeare). The attachment to the word 'sterling' of the qualities of excellence in performance and reliability comes from the use of sterling silver coins, which dates back to the 12th century AD.

The Gold and Silver Connection

Silver's role in the marketplace has been a longstanding mystery. The nature of its relationship with Gold was once obvious to every man, woman and child.

The mystery is easily resolved by the same trip back to ancient Egypt that was taken so fruitfully in the unveiling of the story of money. The origins and role of silver in the marketplace parallel and compliment that of Gold. The relationship between them was formed almost from the first moment they were both mined.

It was not until the Egyptians began to mine far and wide that they discovered that Gold was usually accompanied by an abundance of silver. This was not so in Egypt, though the Wadi Hammamat geologic map mentioned previously casts some doubt on this commonly stated belief. Whenever and wherever it was that it was realised that silver was reliably found alongside Gold and that it had similar properties, then silver became a part of the same process of deity identification.

As the Moon attended the Sun, so silver attended Gold. In the manner that Gold had been accorded the supreme status of sacred representative of the Sun, so silver was accorded the status of sacred representative of the Moon. The conquistadors recorded that the Incas had made Gold and silver representatives of the same celestial bodies[**].

[**]   They poetically named Gold 'the sweat of the sun' (el sudor del sol) and silver 'the tears of the moon' (las lagrimas de la luna).

The Surrogate Money

In the Egyptian New Kingdom, when Gold first began to perform its commercial roles, it was silver that was mostly used in the marketplace. Remember, according to the Egyptologist Nicholas Reeves, it was both Gold and silver that were the primary targets of the tomb-robbers. Gold, in its dignified and supreme role of store of stable value, has always been unsuitable for day-to-day commerce. Practically its value has been too high.

On this one factor alone, ignoring all the other evidence, it is quite clear that Gold did not emerge as money because of its supposed property as the most marketable good. It is not suited for the everyday marketplace and never has been. Far from being the most marketable good, Gold is neither a good nor, because of the high value that even the smallest coin represents, is it very marketable (useful in the everyday marketplace).

From the earliest times of Gold's emergence into the marketplace, silver has acted as Gold's surrogate. This was born of silver's trusted and unique spiritual relationship with Gold and made practical by its lesser value.

This long association and greater utility meant that silver has been what people carried in their pockets when going about their day-to-day business. If there is anything that falls into the category of most marketable good, then it is silver; not because of the machinations of markets, but because of its association with the moon and thus the Sun deity.

Without the availability of silver, it is improbable in the extreme that Gold could have made the leap to the marketplace and impacted so mightily circa 1500 BC. Gold's value was too high; it was only silver, joined at the celestial hip to Gold, which could act on Gold's behalf. The silver that came out of Nubia and the tombs was of the utmost importance to the illustrious future of Gold. Silver has always done the heavy lifting in the marketplace. Simply put, it is far more practical to carry silver coins than Gold coins.

The major monetary metal in history is silver, not Gold.

Milton Friedman

Lacking the definition of money, Mr. Friedman's error, which has been widely shared, is understandable. Gold is the only money, but silver has been its highly visible and irreplaceable surrogate in day-to-day transactions.

The Importance of Silver

The fact that there is only this one chapter on silver should in no way be construed as a diminishment of its importance. Were it not for silver, it is inconceivable that Gold's stability of value could have made the transition to the commercial realm and transported humanity into the modern world. The fact that Gold's value was far too high for day-to-day transactions would have forever consigned its stability of value to dark and dusty temple duties and ceremonial occasions. It was only the utilisation of silver that allowed Gold to migrate to the marketplace.

'A useful value in the everyday marketplace' is legitimately one of the requirements of money. Gold has never effectively satisfied that requirement, but silver has done so admirably on Gold's behalf. Generally speaking there is a clear division of monetary labour. Gold performs the role of 'a known value' in accumulations and silver performs the secondary role as the measure of value in the exchange of goods. The roles are not mutually exclusive.

By virtue of its useful value in the marketplace, silver satisfies the nine requirements of money even better than Gold. This is just another of the blessings of the remarkable monetary duo. Silver's usefulness rests entirely upon Gold's stability of value, but Gold could not have made the transition to the commercial world without the irreplaceable support of silver. The relationship between Gold and silver has been wholly symbiotic. Neither could have attained commercial success without the other and the world would still be trudging along in the poverty of barter and trade goods.

The Gold—Silver Ratio

The Egyptians decreed that Gold was 13.3 times more valuable than silver on the basis that for each cycle of the Sun there were 13.3 cycles of the Moon. That ratio was still in existence when the first coins were produced in Lydia over 800 years later. Silver had much religious significance as the holy representative of the Moon, and very little, if any, value as a good. Like Gold, it also had an increasing stock-to-flow ratio. In consequence, its value was very stable, which is why the 13.3 to 1 ratio held so well for so long, though we have no way of knowing to what degree the marketplace adhered to this official ratio. Over time, silver's religious significance has diminished, at the same time as its value as a good has increased. All subsequent attempts to dictate fixed ratios of value between Gold and silver have failed.

In the modern world of electronics, antibiotics and superconductivity, silver's importance as a good grows ever greater. Along with that come ever-greater fluctuations in its value.

While silver's value tends to drift upwards and downwards, prior to the increased market control exercised by governments during the late 19th and the 20th century, it never strayed far from a 12—17 to 1 ratio with Gold. This is why, despite that fact that it is not an absolute store of stable value, it is close enough to one to be desired in the marketplace. Of course, everyone would prefer Gold, but nobody would turn down silver in its absence.

This crucial relationship between Gold and silver is confirmed by their stock-to-flow ratios. While the readily available stocks of all other metals are measured in weeks, or at most a few months, the stocks of both Gold and silver are measured in decades. And still their stocks continue to grow, though Gold's growth is proportionally greater. While silver's industrial usage is increasing, it is still only a percentage of what is mined ... the flow. Over the decade from 2001 to 2010 silver's average industrial and photographic usage represented just over 62% of mine supply.

Slightly less than 38% was added to the readily available stock in the form of jewellery, silverware, coins, medallions and bullion.

In 2012 alone, 299 million ounces of silver (9300 tonnes) were added to this stock (38% of total annual production of 787 million ounces)[***].

———❦———

The only way that the use of Gold and silver in the marketplace can founder is if there is an artificially fixed ratio of values between the two. There can never be a completely stable relationship between Gold and silver, or between Gold and any other good.

The dominant factor in silver's value is defined by its relationship with Gold, but market forces have an influence. Fluctuations in the ratio are very modest and spread over sufficient time to be easily adaptable to by markets. History demonstrates clearly that without the coercive interference of governments, silver always retains sufficient stability of value to be welcome as Gold's surrogate. Until we experience a free market in money over a sustained period, how much stability and at about what ratio will have to remain conjecture.

No other good possesses silver's stability of value. Silver, with poise and aplomb, manages to straddle the two value paradigms of Gold's stability and goods' instability. In a way it is incorrect to think of silver as either a good or money. It's role is as unique as Gold's.

———❦———

The Hybrid

The concepts of money and goods are inextricably linked, yet quite distinct. Silver does not appear to be either, but yet displays characteristics of both. It is not money because it is valued in terms of Gold, but neither is

---

[***]   Silver Institute

it a simple good because throughout history it has been used to purchase goods in the marketplace and to that degree is the measure of value. How can silver straddle both ends of the stability of value spectrum, occupying the category of both measure and measured?

Is it possible that silver first entered the marketplace as money; on an equal but lesser-valued footing as Gold? It is indisputable that 3,500 years later that situation no longer exists. Today, silver's value as measured by Gold is far from stable; it moves up and down on a daily basis.

Could it be that silver's rising use in the manufacturing process levered it out of a former monetary status? That logic is largely negated by the fact that silver's primary industrial use is in electronics and photography and this did not really begin until the 20th century. The instability of its ratio with Gold long preceded that. It is also discounted by the fact that Gold also had increased use as a good over the same period, yet suffered no damage to its stability of value.

If silver ever were a store of stable value then it is more likely that centuries of manipulation by governments has damaged and distorted silver's role[****]. No matter the cause, the fact exists that the agreement that silver has a stable value and is thus money, if it ever existed, has been long broken.

If silver were now a store of stable value, then it would be possible to peg it to Gold. It is, after all, possible to have a peg between two measures. Both a gallon and a litre measure volumes of liquid. Because they are both stable measures, they have a ratio between them that is precise and unchanging. Silver, being a good whose value is subject to the changing perceptions of the market, is not a measure. It is, like all other goods, measured ... by Gold.

[****]   Apart from artificial Gold to silver ratios imposed by governments, silver was officially 'demonetized' in Germany in 1871 and the US in 1873.

Silver's failure as a store of stable value is more than offset by:

a. its venerable and traditional alignment with Gold's fundamental monetary value and,

b. its long and well known successful history as a very practical monetary surrogate.

While Gold is the only store of stable value, it is silver that is most practical in the marketplace. The difficulties that governments down through the ages have had with setting an arbitrary ratio between the two is explained above, and demonstrated below.

If country A sets a ratio of 15 to 1, silver to Gold, but country B sets a ratio of 14 to 1, silver to Gold, then the silver in country A is going to flood to country B where it will be exchanged for Gold. This Gold will then leave country B and head back to country A where it will be exchanged for silver and the process repeated. Within a very short time, country A will have a shortage of silver coins in circulation and country B will have a shortage of Gold coins in circulation [*****]. An artificial monetary ratio will cause even more distortions than the mispricing of individual goods.

The above situations have happened over and over again. Attempts by governments to fix ratios between Gold and silver, have resulted in failure. This is because only Gold is money and no amount of academic debate or political legislation will ever change that.

Trying to peg the value of one to the other cannot be done. Gold is money and is therefore the measure of value; silver is not money, it is a monetary surrogate. The individual market participants determine silver's ratio with Gold, and while it can be known that the ratio will change from time to time, the changes will be of only a minor nature. It can also be known that with a market-determined ratio, neither the Gold nor silver coins will be disappearing from circulation.

——— ✕✕✕ ———

[*****]   This is paraphrasing an example given by Professor Antal E. Fekete in one his lectures.

For a variety of reasons, including a supposed silver shortage and its ever increasing industrial use and potential, some have predicted that it could reach the same value, or even surpass that of Gold.

That will not happen.

Were the ratio between Gold and silver to become even close to 1 to 1, then silver's venerable existence as a monetary surrogate would come to an end. It is only its lesser value that breathes the life of monetary surrogacy into silver.

In the event that silver's value did begin to approach that of Gold, then it would revert to just another good without any special stature. At that point, the vast stocks of silver would ensure that its price would plummet. Silver is in the paradoxical situation where the very fact of its perceived value rising too high would cause its value to crash. This is hypothetical, for having ascertained silver's true role in its relationship with Gold, and in accordance with a long tradition, we can have confidence that silver will continue marching side-by-side with Gold into the monetary future.

<hr/>

The suggestion has been made that silver will not return to its traditional role as a monetary surrogate, either because there is not enough silver, or because it is no longer necessary. The first point is invalid due to silver's ever increasing stock-to-flow ratio. While it is impossible to ever know how much stock there really is of either Gold or silver, such evidence as there is suggests that the silver stock is almost as understated as the Gold stock. People have been hiding their Gold and silver from governments for thousands of years. A shortage of silver in the marketplace cannot be construed as a shortage of silver. It simply means that it is not available for the paper money being offered.

The second point is in reference to the situation that in the modern era we no longer need silver as a monetary surrogate. We can now weigh Gold down to micrograms. The insertion of these weights into the centre of copper coins means that Gold could cover all aspects of monetary needs. New technologies are already appearing that would allow the practical circulation of Gold measured down to fractions of a gram[******].

There is an observable and comfortable continuity in the relationship between Gold and silver though; they pair as naturally in our minds and language as in the marketplace. This suggests that silver will continue to perform its traditional and honoured role as the surrogate money in the marketplaces of the world. The more salient point is that silver is still considered by the people to be a monetary metal—otherwise its stock-to-flow ratio would have seen its value collapse.

Sitting unobtrusively underneath this whole subject is the concept of exchange. Were it not for the imperative to exchange, the concepts of money and goods would have no meaning. While it seemed irrelevant, a little foray into the area turned up a figurative Gold mine.

[******]   Valaurum

CHAPTER FIFTEEN
EXCHANGE

'The study of money, above all other fields in economics, is
one in which complexity is used to disguise truth or to evade
truth, not to reveal it.'

John Kenneth Galbraith

This new understanding of Gold and money and the precise mechanics of the exchange of goods has many ramifications, including some that were previously considered unrelated to the monetary sphere. Yet, along with this tug into the future, there is an equally compelling demand for an inspection of one other concept that existed prior to the emergence of money—exchange.

An exchange is to give one thing and receive another. Do marketplace exchanges have a commonality with exchanges in other aspects of life and if so, is it pertinent to the story of money?

The fundamental need and ability to exchange with each other is the basis of all interconnected human activity. This imperative to exchange is the reason that humans congregate—the only reason. The positive actions of exchange, including procreation, laughter, friendship, food, security, communication and goods, are the essence of human groups. All human groups can be viewed as an aggregation of exchanges.

What is it that has lain behind the failure to give more than a superficial and cursory glance at the subject of money? Why has such an important area been neglected to the degree that the word could not even be sensibly defined? It was likely borne of the failure to grasp and explore the vital concept of exchange in general. Exchanges span the full range of human interactions; the impulse of all sentient life to group is entirely for the purpose of exchange.

Money cannot be understood except in the context of the whole human condition; it is not a separate entity in isolation from the jigsaw of life. It has been the study of money as though it were divorced from all other human activity that has allowed economics to continue on its confused and ultimately dangerous path. It has seemed a subject separate from the lives of normal people and therefore of little interest, but the decisions made by economists impact on the lives of almost everyone on the planet.

Money is what distinguishes a society from a tribe. Money is the ultimate mechanism for one of the most important of all exchanges— possibly the most important. Trade bridges the divide between the peoples of the world, even when the two parties involved in the exchange are not able to speak each other's language and have little cultural similarity. The utilisation of money increases the ease of these trades exponentially. What was imponderably difficult and able to be achieved by only skilled traders became, with the measure of value, available to anyone, and at light-speed. Money is the super tool of exchange.

--- ∞ ---

Tribal Prejudice

A free market would unite the world's people volitionally. The efforts by governments to force an unnatural unity via political amalgamations such as the European Union, and by inappropriate migration, will continue to be more and more counter-productive. It is their own paper money enforced by their own legal tender laws that is fragmenting societies back to their constituent tribal parts.

It is accumulations of money that allow the creation of wealth. Without accumulations, prosperity can only be achieved by stealing from other tribes or by depriving them of access to hunting grounds—or, its 21st century equivalent, energy supplies. The simple process of adding money into the equation utterly changes this tribal dynamic. Money displays the commonality of all people for everyone to see and understand. It shows and facilitates a way of achieving future security without the risk of death and destruction. It allows a gentler existence based on mutual self-betterment.

In its absence, ancient tribal enmities will always come to the fore. The imposition by legislative force of a 'love thy neighbour' agenda is made redundant by circulating money. Moralizing preachers, especially those armed with guns instead of reason, will never be as powerful a force as self-interest.

Tribes, with their alienation from other people and tribes, are the antithesis of society. In the presence of money, goods are the representation of the core values of each and every individual without exception. When the truly free market manufactures goods, it is indifferent to the culture, rank, colour, religion, sexual preference or personal beliefs of the potential recipients. The free market is only interested in the flow of money.

If there is sufficient concentration of demand for specific goods to satisfy core values, then the free market will supply them—quickly and without qualms. What those core values are is of no relevance. Gold is the great equaliser.

The world of goods chasing Gold is profoundly different from the world of paper money chasing goods.

Prejudice is a product of tribal existence; it is born of the necessity to identify with and support aspects of one's own tribe—to show solidarity. At a crude (pre money) level of existence, this is perceived as a survival mechanism. As the world has moved further and further away from Gold so these old prejudices have begun to again rear their ugly heads. Laws can temporarily smother them, but they cannot stop the inevitable and natural reversion to tribal alienations. With money in circulation these manifestations are counter-productive and quickly fade. They work against prosperity and future security.

The tribal mentality is preoccupied, sometimes obsessed, with any signs of deviation from the proper and traditional ways of the tribe. It is a way of existence tending toward conflict and intolerance.

Society is preoccupied with producing goods that are needed, wanted and can be afforded by those with the core values to match. What the recipients look like or believe is of little interest. It is a way of existence tending toward peaceful trade and tolerance.

The free market circulation of Gold is intolerant of prejudice.

Money takes the every day tribal exchanges of semen, food and security etc. and raises it to the level of complex exchange. Complex exchange is another way of saying 'circulating money'. Society is properly defined:

'An enduring state of harmonious, widespread and complex exchange.'

——⊗∞⊗——

For all that, money is just another exchange in the vast ocean of exchanges that define human groups and must be studied as such.

Language and money are the ultimate and most sophisticated expressions of this need to exchange; the first is required to exchange concepts, the second to exchange goods. As a language that failed to communicate would hinder the exchange of concepts, so money that failed to store a stable value would hinder the exchange of goods. The primary importance of these exchanges is obliquely acknowledged in the defence of freedom of speech and property rights.

The circulation of Gold and silver creates the highest order of exchange. As exchanges become complex, so, accordingly, do societies become more complex; one begets the other because they are manifestations of the same phenomenon.

The extraordinary rise in the level of commercial exchange created by the circulation of Gold in the 18th and 19th century, brought forth not only the beginnings of material wealth for those who were formerly penniless serfs, but also an outburst of literary and intellectual discourse. A similar process happened in the Egyptian New Kingdom and in the Renaissance of the 15th and 16th centuries. The sophistication of commercial exchange utilizing money encouraged a rise in the efficacy of all other means of exchange.

The creation of surplus goods brings about leisure. It is no coincidence that the finer points of human existence come to the fore in the times of Gold.

The Missing Link

Money has been the missing link in the understanding of social evolution. Without money, there was no possibility of the sophisticated exchanges and wealth accumulations necessary to propel humanity out of tribal groupings. The lack of awareness of the importance of money, even denial in some quarters, is of an even greater order of magnitude than would be the casual dismissal of the value of language or love. The use of trade goods and paper money in the marketplace is the equivalent of grunting and gesticulating in language. It can work, sort of, but Shakespeare would have struggled to make a name for himself.

> The recovery of the past in this larger sense is demanding a new type of investigator—a cosmopolitan student of man, who is alike anthropologist, archaeologist, ethnologist, comparative religionist, versed in art and literature and acquainted both with the classical and the leading oriental languages of antiquity.
>
> James Henry Breasted—Professor of Egyptology and
> Oriental History at the University of Chicago

This quote, though insightful and from one of the acknowledged greats of Egyptology, serves to highlight a constant omission from the analysis of history—what about the monetarist? There can be no understanding of any tribe or society without a study of its exchanges, particularly in the area of trade.

——⊗⊗⊗——

Honest Exchange

The degraded status of paper money, coupled with the confusion caused by the 'Grand Unified Theory' has tainted the whole paradigm. Those who recoil from the fraud and inequities that accompany the use of paper should not make the mistake of transferring that distaste over to Gold. As much as paper money brings out the worst of humanity, so Gold brings out the best. The finest traits of humanity can only flourish in the presence of honest exchange.

A person's social level matches their ability and willingness to honestly exchange. A hermit has no human exchanges and is unsocial. There is also the person who resides in society but takes money or goods without exchange; this is the criminal. Such a person is worse than just unsocial; he or she is anti-social. A society is lost to the degree that anti-social people come to dominate it.

The person who honestly exchanges across the full spectrum of human existence, family, friends, activities and work, is expressing the highest degree of socialness. As a by-product, and all other things being equal, they will achieve the highest degree of personal happiness.

——⊗⊗⊗——

Once the process of exchange has formed groups, then a further level of behaviour becomes in evidence. Qualities such as compassion, generosity, courtesy and kindness are unique to, and arise from, the individual. Yet these noble qualities are meaningless without a recipient, without the presence of others. For them to come into existence, exchange must have previously formed a group. Without it, these qualities must remain merely dormant potential.

The qualities are magnified with each increase in exchange.

The complex exchange of circulating Gold and silver that transforms tribes into societies greatly enhances this process. While these virtues require no exchange, indeed that is their virtue, they obviously cannot exist prior to it. The greater the level of exchange, the greater is the evidence of these virtues. In England, the ultra-sophistication of circulating Gold coin transformed court etiquette into the ordinary person's common courtesy (good manners); it also institutionalised the concept of charity and 'good works'. Respected charities such as The Red Cross (British branch), The Salvation Army and Dr. Barnardo's Home for orphans were a by-product of the circulation of Gold and silver in the UK in the 19th century. Compassion was both voluntary and genuine. The productive people who had gained so much from money donated to those less fortunate. The underlying theme was having a consideration for others.

All indications suggest that this level of virtuous behaviour is directly proportional to the degree of exchange that underpins it. The curtailment and degradation of any exchanges, let alone the primary exchanges, must result in the diminishment of not only the finest qualities of the individual, but of society itself. The complete freedom to exchange in all areas of life, but most importantly in the area of trade, is the pre-condition for the advancement of the human race.

Once exchange has moved from its tribal beginnings to its fully evolved state of complex exchange, then it has been referred to as a civilization. The word 'civilization' is derived from 'civil', which introduces an element of confusion. It insinuates that complex exchange can only be achieved with the presence of government. So far our history has shown this to be the opposite of the truth. What has been termed civilization is simply society: the ultimate manifestation of money in circulation and accumulation. For clarity's sake it is best termed as such.

Gold moors humanity to not only an honest and workable monetary system, but to a decent and just existence. Its replacement with paper money does not merely allow the baser actions of humanity; by the distortions and manipulations made necessary by paper's lack of stability and honesty, it very effectively encourages them. When money is at the centre of society, dishonest and indecent behaviour are not of course eliminated, but they are minimised and exposed, which allows for their easy identification and social condemnation.

When the connection between money and communication and social wellbeing is not understood at the level of the individual, it hinders his or her survival; when it is legislatively violated at the level of governments, it is calamity and ruin in the making.

Withdrawing circulating Gold and silver from the exchange of goods is the equivalent of withdrawing circulating verbs and nouns from the exchange of concepts.

The money gained from an abundance of surplus goods creates the leisure necessary for the development and appreciation of the arts. This raises the necessity for sophisticated language even further. The creation, evolvement and maintenance of societies are all dependent on sophisticated ways of exchanging. The great plays of Shakespeare emerged in the period following the reintroduction of sterling silver coins by Edward VI in 1551. The world's great philosophers have reliably emerged from the times of wealth created by circulating Gold and silver.

Above a rudimentary level* it is circulating money that precedes the development of language. If that speculation were to remain valid, then the reverse would also have to be true. The removal of money in

---

* At the most basic level of exchange the only language is that of the hunt and similar group activities. At the tribal level the sophistication of language increases, but it is only with the advent of society that a peak of sophisticated communication emerges.

the early 20ᵗʰ century would have to have been followed by a widespread decline in the standard of literacy. It is hard to argue that this was not the case. Correlation is not necessarily causation, but it is an interesting point to note.

Conflict

It is money and language that sit at the base of society. Both must be present, and both must be understandable and understood for humanity to be able to exchange and coexist in a social manner. Society is dependent upon these two indispensable features. If either is weakened, then the natural tendency of humanity to live peacefully will be damaged. The inability to exchange, either goods or ideas, is the precursor to the breakdown of harmony and the onset of the most extreme expression of that anti-social state—war.

War is the degeneration of money and language to the point where the only exchange is that of bullets and blows. Exchange will always happen, but lacking good money and good communication it will not be of a social nature.

Both 'war' and 'peace' are words used to describe the presence of certain phenomena. No proper understanding can come from the use of such words, without an understanding of the underlying conditions. As society is created and enhanced by the ability to freely and honestly exchange (peace), so it is fragmented by the inability to do the same (war).

The continuous wars and ethnic cleansings of the 20ᵗʰ and early 21ˢᵗ centuries are all manifestations of the collapse of society. As the emergence of money launched us out from our tribal beginnings, so its absence inexorably returns us.

The degradation of the primary tools of exchange has brought about the situation of individuals reverting to the notion that they are somehow, in some indefinable way, separated out from everybody else. It is this tribal sense of alienation, an inability to relate to others, that allows for some of humanity's most despicable acts. Only the free and honest exchange of ideas and goods can ignite the unity of humanity. From that unity springs the shared morality, the commonality of purpose and the sense of destiny that further cements the ties.

It was free people who developed both language and money, not governments. Indeed, through their seizure of education and money, governments have caused immense damage to both. The subsequent combination of illiteracy and paper money means that the ability to honestly exchange ideas and goods has been degraded. For that reason the commonality of humanity is no longer apparent to many.

We live in a world where reading and writing above the level of texting is very hard for many, and where what is used as money is fast approaching complete breakdown. We also live in a world that is full of theft, lies, prejudice, immorality, hatred and schisms; where even the family unit is being torn apart. None of these facts are unrelated.

With seven billion people in a world armed to the teeth with weapons of unimaginably destructive power, this is a situation that should be of concern to everyone except the truly mad.

First Things First

There is a school of thought that believes we will only return to Gold once society has raised itself to the necessary moral level. This reverses cause and effect. Without circulating money, decent and social exchanges between individuals, and peaceful coexistence between groups and nations, will continue to be the exception rather than the rule.

Where the common factor of Gold was absent, so too was society. We do not speak of the society of the Australian Aborigine or the Inuit for the reason that they were never elevated by the discovery of Gold's properties.

The primary god of the Mongols was the blue sky; the Sun was worshipped only as a secondary god. They did not accumulate Gold, though they belatedly came to recognize its value in the marketplace. The influence of these militant nomads spanned a vast area, but lacking Gold accumulations they never became a society.

Material values are most clearly displayed in estates. When the Mongol chiefs died they bequeathed land, cattle and slaves, but not Gold. Rather than the Mongol society, we more correctly refer to them as the Mongol horde. Were it the Mongol *hoard* then history would have had a different outcome. The Mongol tribes eventually retreated back to the obscurity of their ancestral homes, or were absorbed by Gold-orientated enduring societies such as the Chinese.

To dismiss money is to dismiss society, for the two are more than just coexistent. As money and language are the cause, society and social behaviour are the effects.

As an aside, a proper understanding of the contiguous relationship between complex exchange and societies gives insight into other concepts. To more properly understand social terms we need to explore what sort of exchange it is based on; e.g. 'friendship' is an exchange of loyalties. A better understanding of exchange produces not just a better understanding of money, but also a better understanding of life in general.

When Gold is dropped into life's pond, its virtues ripple out across the whole span of human existence. When Gold is withdrawn, then societies are not only lessened, they are slowly but surely destroyed.

When people stop trusting money, they stop trusting each other.

Steve Forbes

Chapter Sixteen
Peace in Our Time

In peace sons bury their fathers;
in war fathers bury their sons
King Croesus of Lydia—6th century BC

The exploration of the real story of money touches upon some areas that may have been thought to be quite unrelated, not least of which is its crucial role in the founding of human societies. In the manner that money builds societies, so its removal destroys them. While its relationship with liberty and prosperity is well explored and understood, the connection between money and peace has not been so documented or clear.

All sane people desire world peace, but a history of seemingly endless wars has made the idea seem Utopian—so far-fetched as to be almost impossible.

There is supporting evidence for this grim view; the wars not only continue, they grow both in number and in terms of the potential for destruction. Chemical and nuclear weapons cannot be restricted to the battleground, nor is there any effort to do so. Drones patrol the skies. Space based weapons systems are in an advanced state of development, as are fully autonomous killer robots.

Is war unstoppable? Is human nature so depraved that we are forever doomed to see our children marching off to distant lands to kill or be killed, or to maim or be maimed? Even those who emerge physically unharmed are psychologically scarred for life. By the time US troop departed Iraq at the end of 2011, suicides were higher than combat deaths. The financial pain is also severe. Estimates of the US debt from the Iraq and Afghani wars range from four to six trillion dollars. Assuming the middle ground, that is $15,000 for every American man, woman and child. Nobody really gains from the experience of war. The subject of peace requires a closer inspection if a realistic answer to whether it is achievable is to be arrived at. There is little point in working for peace, if a state of war truly is human nature.

In the search for the reasons for war, one of the most important questions is: who starts them? Why would parents en masse demand that their children go off to fight to the death with the children of other parents?

Well of course, they don't. People don't declare a state of war; that is what governments do.

History records no examples of people clamouring for war against the people of other nations, other than after they had been whipped into a frenzy of hostility by government propaganda.

The first thing to be understood about international wars is that governments instigate them, not people. War is not human nature; war is government nature. Do psychopathic individuals exist? Yes, but not to any great degree. They seem numerous because of the preoccupation of the media with them. The newspapers are full of the doings of psychopaths—our lives are not. In truth, the vast majority of humanity is composed of well-meaning, decent people just trying to do the best for themselves and their families.

An important question is: how can governments afford to fight wars? This is where the line of reasoning becomes interesting and leads to another question; has the world ever known peace?

—⁂—

The Hundred Years Peace

From 1815 to 1914, the incessant beating of the military drums finally died down. The world experienced only seven wars of note in the 19th century. The largest was the American Civil War with total casualties of around 600,000. The Napoleonic wars that preceded this period alone produced casualty figures of somewhere between 3,500,000 and 6,500,000.

In *The Great Transformation* (1944), Karl Polanyi famously referred to the 19th century as 'the Hundred Years Peace'.

Why were there one hundred years of relative peace in the period 1815 to 1914? What happened—and what happened to change it back again? Why was the most peaceful century in recorded world history followed by the most brutally destructive—'The Hundred Years War' of the 20th century.

Twelve years after the end of the Napoleonic wars in 1815, England made its Gold standard official. By the early 1870s, most of Europe had done the same because they could not compete without it. The 'fierce and unresolved debate*' as to why England's industrial and financial leadership slipped in the last thirty years of the 19th century is easily explained from the point of view that when England had a near monopoly on banknotes redeemable for Gold it was supreme; when it didn't it wasn't. At the turn of the 20th century, the fifty most prosperous countries in the world were using either circulating Gold, paper banknotes backed by Gold, or a combination of both.

In 1914, the European governments beginning with Germany, France, Belgium and England, abandoned Gold. Bank notes were no longer redeemable for anything. The match of dates and subsequent events was not coincidence.

—❊❊❊—

*   Peter Wisher *The Pound in Your Pocket*

The Money of the People

It is often noted that Gold is the money of the people, but any sort of supporting logic for the statement is usually absent. In a democracy with circulating Gold, it is the people who have control of the money. Governments cannot print Gold; if they wish to make war then they have to tax the people to pay for it. As already discussed, people do not want war and will rarely vote for it—especially when the cost is not only their children's blood, but when it is apparent that the monetary cost will be extracted from their pockets.

The only European wars of the one hundred years peace were the Prussian wars, first against Austria then France. They were made possible by the fact that Prussia was not a democracy, which meant that the people had no say in the matter. Even so, the restrictions of Gold meant that the wars lasted only seven days and eight months respectively.

In the interests of waging war and for no other reason, governments abandoned Gold in 1914 and began printing paper money un-backed by anything except the good faith and trust that we are supposed to have in politicians. All sorts of other reasons were given for abandoning Gold; all were just propaganda to justify this most egregious of crimes; the wholesale slaughter of the young of Europe—paid for by their parents.

The people of Europe were very relaxed about the threat of war in 1914; until war was declared it had not even been on the front pages of the newspapers. It was understood that if worst came to worst, governments would be unable to send their people to fight beyond a few months as they did not have the Gold to pay for it.

War is very expensive.

The abandonment of Gold, with the instatement of paper in its place, changed everything. A 'few months' became four years, with a military and civilian death toll of over 17,000,000. The 'flower of a generation' was wiped out. If the enormity and significance of that terrible figure is hard to grasp, then consider the situation in terms of something more emotionally neutral. The volumes of global trade that preceded 1914 were not achieved again until the 1970s. By that one yardstick the world was set back sixty years; in human terms the cost was and remains incalculable. Society began its retreat.

Europe was ruined. No such widespread devastation had been witnessed since the monetary degradation of the Thirty Year war, three hundred years earlier.

It is difficult, if not impossible, to separate the urge of governments to debase the coinage, from the urge to go to war. The two go hand-in-hand; over and over again this pattern of monetary debasement by governments to finance war dominates history.

Nostalgia For Gold

After the Great War of 1914 to 1918, Europe looked back wistfully to the pre-war period. The Hungarians referred to it as 'Békebeli idók'—the 'Peaceful Times'. In France, the peace and prosperity of the pre war era had allowed not only technological and medical developments, but also wonderful advances in the visual arts, theatre, literature and music. Haute Couture fashion was created. The French name for this period was *La Belle Époque*—'The Beautiful Era'. The English called it simply 'The Golden Age'; the age when, for the first time in recorded history, working people gained access to schooling and home-ownership.

It was left to Stefan Zweig, the peerless Austrian writer, to poignantly describe the period best in his 1942 autobiography *Die Welt von Gestern* (The World of Yesterday)[**]. No one could read Zweig's book and not understand that he wrote about a superior age; an age of the arts, and of liberty, prosperity and peace.

[**]   Stefan Zweig and his wife Lotte Altmann committed suicide the day after the manuscript was sent to the publisher. Their despair at the loss of The Golden Age and of the return to tribalism was very personal. They were Jews.

The 20th century was one of war and brutality such as the world had never witnessed. Far from ceasing after the Great War—'the war to end wars', the savagery intensified. It began with the Russian and Spanish Civil wars; then World War Two came and went with more deaths than all previous wars combined. This was followed by the crushing of Eastern Europe under Soviet tank tracks, the Chinese civil war, the Korean war, Vietnam war, Cambodian war, India/Pakistan war, The Soviet/Afghan war, the Iran/Iraq war, the Persian Gulf war and the Balkans war. Unknown millions of lives were snuffed out in the paper money wars of the 20th century.

The word 'genocide' did not exist until the 20th century.

2014 was the centenary of the loss of the Golden Age. Those one hundred years of peace are now precisely one hundred years past. How many more centuries will it be before the people recreate those times? Governments will never of their own initiative hand back their self-granted monopoly to print money. The extremes and abuses of government power stem directly from their ability to create and debase the money supply.

To return to the question: 'how can governments afford wars?'—the answer is that they abolish real money and put in its place paper money—debt. They then begin to print ... and print and print, until the debt is so humongous that even the interest cannot be paid, never mind the principal. Welcome to the modern world. Any discussion of peace has to include the subject of money.

War and government control of money are inseparable.

Endless money forms the sinews of war

Marcus Tullius Cicero

With more primitive weapons this situation, though tragic at the level of the individual and family, was tolerable. Today, with government control of weapons of unimaginably destructive power, a situation exists that is intolerable. The world is living with the threat of literal annihilation. The ultimate 'power to the people' is circulating Gold and silver.

Gold in use as day-to-day money has many advantages; none is as important as the constraint that it places upon the ability of governments to wage wars.

There will be no general peace again in this world until we abolish paper money. When Gold is in circulation then it is trade, not war, which is the preoccupation of humanity. Trade is peaceful and beneficial; war is violent and evil. Which of these futures do we want for our children?

A government not constrained by honest money will eventually send their people to war. There can be no talk of peace in our time until such talk is accompanied by the insistent demand of the public for circulating Gold.

Peace is not a Utopian dream; peace is the natural state of a free people using honest money.

Chapter Seventeen
Las Indias

Get gold, humanely if possible-but at all hazards, get gold.
King Ferdinand of Spain—1511

Flowers Are Our Only Garments

Flowers are our only garments,
only songs make our pain subside,
diverse flowers on earth,
Ohuaya ohuaya.
Perhaps my friends will be lost,
my companions will vanish
when I lie down in that place, I Yoyontzin *-Ohuaye!-*
in the place of song and of Life Giver,
Ohuaya ohuaya.
Does no one know where we are going?
Do we go to God's home or
do we live only here on earth?
Ah ohuaya.
Let your hearts know,
oh princes, oh eagles and jaguars
that we will not be friends forever,
only for a moment here, then we go
to Life Giver's home,
Ohuaya ohuaya.

By Nezahualcoyotl (Aztec poet)*

* My sincere thanks to John Curl for both his translation and the permission to publish

The words of King Ferdinand of Spain carried more weight than those of Nezahualcoyotl; less humanity, less humility, less grace and less beauty, but more weight.

Spain and Central/South America were separated by not only a vast ocean, but by tradition, morality and language. The only value that they had in common was the Gold constant. The local skills in refining and exquisitely shaping the soft metal of the gods gave no protection against hard Spanish steel.

The conquistadors destroyed the great tribes of Las Indias. They murdered, raped, betrayed and pillaged. They stole everything of value that they could lay their hands on, but mostly they stole Gold and silver. The cupidity of the Spanish knew no bounds; honest exchange was non-existent. The justification was that the Indians were bloodthirsty savages who sacrificed innocent victims to their gods. This was, without a doubt, history's most egregious example of the pot calling the kettle black. It exceeded the savagery of the annihilation of Carthage and Corinth by the Romans in 146 BC.

An Aztec observer of the Spanish Gold grab said:

> The Spaniards burst into smiles; their eyes shone with pleasure. They picked up the gold and fingered it like monkeys. They seemed to be transported by joy as if their hearts were illuminated and made new. The truth is that they longed and lusted for gold. Their bodies welled up with greed and their hunger was ravenous. They hungered like pigs for that gold.

The survivors were reduced to poverty; their sciences, languages and even their religion were lost forever as they were forced to worship the god of their conquerors. The Spanish not only murdered millions of people[***], they razed whole cities and temples and even dug up graves

---

[**]   Axtell, James. Beyond 1492: Encounters in Colonial North America. New York: Oxford UP, 1992.

[***]   *Rivers of Blood, Rivers of Gold* by Mark Cocker states ' ... eleven million indigenous Americans lost their lives in the first eight years following the Spanish invasion of Mexico. In the Andean empire of the Incas the figure was more than eight million.' The Aztec people of Mexico and the Incas of South America were wiped from the face of the Earth.

in their search for Gold and silver. They obliterated some of the most unique tribal societies that the world has ever seen. The Central/South Americans never recovered their lands, dignity or Gold. Only scattered remnants of the tribes, including some ruins and poignant poetry, remain.

The artistic Gold and silver ornaments were melted down and shipped off to Europe. The Spanish were ruthlessly efficient; very little was successfully hidden. The destruction of the societies continued for three centuries. Those who survived, and who had once lived in great cities, were reduced to living in the jungle. The ruined cities and temples became overgrown with vegetation and it was almost as if their history had never been.

—⚬⚬⚬—

Malinvestments

In the same way that the cheap credit provided by central banks exacerbated malinvestments in the 20th and 21st centuries, so did the shipload after shipload of stolen Gold[****] and silver arriving in Spain in the 16th century. Easy money or credit is always a disturbing incentive. Labour

---

[****]   Modern marine archaeology has noted that the cargoes coming out of Las Indias were much larger than official records show (The Funnel of Gold—Mendel Peterson). At first the Crown took 50% of all Gold and silver landed at Seville (after 1717 the official port of entry was changed to Cadiz). This was gradually reduced as it became obvious that the disincentive created by the percentage outweighed the gain. Eventually the Crown settled on 20%. This Crown percentage was, as throughout all empires and millennia, an inducement to greatly understate the amounts. Unknown quantities of Gold were siphoned off into private hoards. The smuggling of Gold increased substantially from 1600 onwards.

Antonio Vazquez de Espinosa was a Carmelite friar who travelled in the Americas in the early 17th century. With reference to the enormous silver deposits at the Potosi range in Upper Peru (now Bolivia) he asserted that at least as much of the silver was hidden from the Crown as was received.

became in short supply ***** as people signed up to sail to the new world. Wages were higher on the Gold galleons than they were back home. Productive capital was reemployed from farming and manufacturing to shipbuilding. More money could be made by plundering Gold and silver, than by manufacturing goods and tilling fields. This was made especially true in the latter case because the tax burden fell unduly heavily on the agricultural sector.

Spain's whole economy became skewed.

John Kenneth Galbraith ****** stressed the point that once the plundering of the worked Gold was finished, much of the Gold and silver was mined. The implication being that this was not the same as looting. When a majority of the labour costs are neutralised by slavery, then this still amounts to looting. Theft is theft, whether it is of labour or property.

The stolen Gold was a complete disaster for Spain, but because of the many misunderstandings surrounding Gold and money, the nature of the disaster has been misinterpreted. The Spanish booty brought about not only the collapse of two societies; it brought terminal confusion to the profession of economics.

It was because of the erroneous interpretations of this event that the deeply flawed 'quantity theory of money' became cemented into place. It was an attempt to prove that prices would rise or fall based on an increase or decrease in the quantity of whatever was called money. The idea took hold and was (and is) repeated ad infinitum. It is a cornerstone of The Grand Unified Theory. This was the nail in the coffin for future economic reality. A store of stable value can never cause such a phenomenon.

***** At its peak the fleet consisted of 50 galleons. Each galleon had a crew of approximately 200 men. 10,000 of the most able-bodied men were extracted from a population of only nine million. This shortage of labour was greatly exacerbated by the need for soldiers to fight the numerous wars that the Gold allowed the Kings of Spain to wage.

****** *Money—Whence it Came, Where it Went* 1975

It was here that the Frankenstein monetary theory that rose to manhood in the 20th century was born.

About one hundred years after the first galleons had set sail, the rise in general prices in Spain was around 300%*******. Many of the goods that were once locally manufactured and much of the food that had once been locally grown, now had to be imported. The need for more and more imports saw prices rise and poverty begin to take hold. Even many of the goods and provisions for the galleons embarking on the three to six months trip to Las Indias had to be imported. The ships bringing these goods from Italy, England, Germany and France mingled with the mighty transatlantic fleet of Spanish galleons prior to their spring and autumn departures. The marauding English and French pirates dictated a policy of strength in numbers.

As the Gold available to be stolen began to dwindle in amounts, so the cargoes became almost solely silver. Eventually, this too began to run out and the grand fleets were reduced to a trickle.

In Spain meanwhile, opulent lifestyles, but mostly government wars, had seen the Gold flow out of the country. What little remained was in the lavishly decorated churches and cathedrals. What also remained was the inability of the country to meet its own basic needs. The wealth gained from expropriation and that from production look very similar in the short-term. Even the arts and literature flourished during this period, as did the charitable institutions for the less fortunate. These are some of the themes common to all times of Gold.

The difference between stolen wealth and produced wealth only becomes apparent in the longer term.

Wealth creation, the growth that stems from accumulation, can continue indefinitely; wealth expropriation can only continue until the victims either cannot or will not give any more. In the case of Las Indias it was the former. Gradually the easily accessible Gold and silver diminished;

******* *Papers on the Economic History of Spain*—Earl Hamilton. As shocking as this figure sounds, it is worth noting that it is only a small fraction of the general price rise in the US over the last 100 years.

as it did, so began the slow decline of what was by now the Spanish pseudo-economy. Lacking the underpinning of surplus production it collapsed. They lost their colonies; they lost everything. Their society was destroyed, though not as thoroughly as those of Las Indias.

The one element, other than common sense and morality, which informed of the unsustainable nature of the situation, was the huge gap between the 'haves' and 'have-nots' in Spain. At one end of the social divide was wealth beyond imagination; at the other were the growing ravages of extreme poverty. Tramps, beggars, pickpockets, thieves and prostitutes swarmed the cities of Spain. No such broad wealth disparity can last long in a society that practices honest exchange.

The rise in prices was brought about by malinvestments as a result of King Ferdinand's ill-fated 'get rich quick' scheme.

The Other Side of the Coin

It is instructive to contemplate how different the story would have been if, instead of pillaging, the Spanish had been prepared to trade with Las Indias. They could have signed an exclusive trade agreement. The need for trade items would have resulted in a substantial increase in the need for Spanish made goods. New factories would have been needed, which would have increased work in construction and manufacturing. New ships (with a more viable, long-term future) would have been needed to accommodate the trade. Builders, sailors and craftsmen would have been in high demand.

Employment would have risen and the wealth and health of the nation would have been enhanced. Smart business people would have made their way to Spain without delay. Other governments would have sought trade rights ... for a Spanish percentage of course. There would have been a substantial increase in the standard of living—on both sides of the Atlantic.

The Indians, for the loss of some of their Gold and silver, would have received wondrous goods that they had not even imagined existed till that time. They would also have been introduced to the sophisticated concept of money, which would have taken their existing store of stable value into a new realm of existence. Both societies would have gained********. It is likely that a more ethical approach to the Gold of Las Indias in the 16th century would have seen the world with a predominantly Hispanic culture in the 21st century.

So King Ferdinand got his Gold, but in so doing, he lost the Spanish their industries, their empire and their prosperity. Unfortunately, due to the usual time lag, the cause and effect of the Spanish disaster has not been well understood. Four hundred years later, the dismally unsound interpretation of the event remains that Spain suffered from a hyperinflation because there was too much Gold.

Dishonesty at the level of the individual or groups ruins individuals or groups. Dishonesty on a grand scale, such as can only happen at the level of government, ruins nations and collapses societies.

It also confuses economists.

******** Rudy Fritsch contributed much of the scenario in the above three paragraphs in an exchange of emails.

CHAPTER EIGHTEEN
WHAT IS THE GOLD STANDARD?

The gold standard) requires nothing else than that the
government abstain from deliberately sabotaging it.

Ludwig von Mises

An improved general understanding of what the Gold standard is would make it harder to sabotage in the future. It would also assist the world to move toward a true Golden age. That the world needs Gold to come out from the hoards and to begin circulating again is beyond question. The chronic application of muddled economic theories, in combination with the taxation mandated use of paper money*, has damaged markets. At the same time, the severity of that damage has also ensured our return to Gold. What cannot be predicted at this point is in what form Gold will be employed.

Sundry commentators labour under the delusion that there can be many different forms of a Gold standard. The impression is often given that 'Gold standard' means whatever the person being interviewed says it means,

---

* Gold and silver cannot currently be used for the purchase of goods without the buy and sell price of the metals being noted. The 'buy' price refers to the time that the metals were first acquired for paper money; the 'sell' price refers to the price of the metals in paper money at the time of the purchase of the goods. The difference has to be declared and is taxed as 'profit'. The cumbersome nature of this makes circulation of the monetary metals impractical.

providing that the word Gold is included somewhere. This is a fallacy in need of correction. What the 'Gold standard' is, is not an opinion, it is a fact ... though a much misunderstood one.

——— ⊗⊗⊗ ———

There is Only One Gold Standard

The confusion around this subject has spanned hundreds of years. It is time that there was a definitive statement as to precisely what the Gold standard is. Fortunately there is and it is available in the dictionary. Apart from the dictionaries' rather dismal attempts in the area of money where they are dependent on the opinions of economists, they can usually be relied on for a trusted judgement.

The dictionary definition of the 'Gold standard' is in complete accord with the discovery of the true definition of Gold as being 'a store of stable value', and of money as being 'a known weight and fineness of Gold'. The problem has not, as would be assumed, been with the many misunderstandings surrounding the word 'Gold' and 'money'. The problem has been with the word 'standard'.

The word 'standard' is not at all a contentious or controversial word. There is no debate swirling through the intellectual ranks as to what the word does or doesn't mean. The word 'standard' has a very precise, accepted and well understood meaning. It is just that people tend to ignore it in the context of the Gold standard. The following are some pertinent extracts from the New Oxford American Dictionary. Other dictionaries will confirm this meaning:

> standard ...
> - 'an idea or thing used as a measure, norm, or model in comparative evaluations : the wages are low by today's standards | the system had become an industry standard.'
> - 'a system by which the value of a currency is defined in terms of gold or silver or both.'

The first extract speaks of a measure. The Gold standard means the 'gold measure'. Gold is the measure of commercial value as surely as a gallon or a litre is the measure of liquid volume. The second extract talks about a currency being defined in terms of Gold. If a currency is defined in terms of Gold then it is defined in terms of the weight and fineness of Gold, not its atomic number or some other attribute. The Gold standard refers to a known weight of .99 Gold as being the measure of value.

Under the classical 'Gold standard' of the 19th century, the US dollar was defined as one twentieth of a Gold ounce; the UK pound as slightly less than one quarter of a Gold ounce. Neither government abided by these restrictions; both circulated ever-greater amounts of paper than they had Gold to represent. No sensible person can deny it was better than the wholesale fraud of the 100% paper standard that it fostered, but it was not the Gold standard.

Any system whereby Gold is measured in terms of euros, yuan, pounds, roubles, yen, dollars or dodos etcetera, or any combination of paper monies, would not be a Gold standard. In that situation, the paper would be the measure and Gold the measured. That would, by definition, be a paper standard. Providing some Gold backing does not transform a paper standard into a Gold standard, it just makes it a better class of paper standard—a hooker wearing Gold bling comes to mind.

A paper representation of money that was 100% backed by a weight of Gold and instantly redeemable for Gold would be the Gold standard, but only if it had on it the weight of the Gold that it represented. For example there could be a 1-gram note, a 2-gram note, a 10-gram note etcetera. Under the Gold standard the notes are not called dollars etcetera, just weights of Gold. Pound, shilling, penny, shekel, dollar, mark etcetera were all originally weights, not just meaningless brand names.

With the wisdom of hindsight it becomes obvious that it was this that allowed the controllers of money to withdraw the Gold. The long association of these brand names with Gold had given them a perception of worth in their own right. People came to forget that the legitimacy of these names rested on the weight of Gold or silver that they represented. Money was spoken about in terms of weights, not abstract numbers. The concept that coinage was valued by its weight and was irrespective of whatever was stamped on the coin survived right up until the late Middle Ages. It was then that the names began to become divorced from the original concept.

To make sure that this is the correct interpretation, the origin of the word 'standard' from the previously mentioned dictionary will also be examined.

> ORIGIN Middle English (denoting a flag raised on a pole as a rallying point, the authorized <u>exemplar of a unit of measurement</u>, or an upright timber): shortening of Old French estendart, from estendre 'extend'; in sense 3, influenced by the verb stand. (author's underline)

So we do have the correct interpretation. A look at the word 'numeraire', again from the same dictionary (though it is confirmed by others) is also instructive ...

> 'An item or commodity acting as a measure of value or as a standard for currency exchange.'

The dictionary, that impartial arbiter of what each individual component of the English language means, proclaims most emphatically, indeed, as being beyond the possibility of debate, that the very essence of the Gold standard is that Gold must be the measure of value. What else could possibly be the measure in any science other than that which had proved to be the most stable?

How did the Gold standard come to be so thoroughly misunderstood, even by some honest money advocates? One could speculate that it was due to the 'usual suspects' ... those involved in the printing of bank notes for which there was insufficient or even no Gold backing. No matter, but it is high time that this destructive misunderstanding, myth, or disinformation, whatever it should be labelled, is finally laid to rest. It is such vagueness of terminology that has allowed the gradual evolvement of the current paper fiasco.

With the Gold standard, it is possible to use paper representations of money, but each piece of paper would have to stand for a weight of Gold that was in existence and that was available to the holder of the note on demand.

While it is possible with the Gold standard to use paper representations of money, governments and central bankers have a long history of cheating by degrading such paper. They have consistently printed more paper than they have Gold to back it and end up severing the link between their paper and Gold completely. All such paper monies become worth only the weight of the paper, not the weight of the Gold they once represented. They move from bank vaults to fireplaces or curiosity shops with predictable regularity.

The best and most practical Gold standard is one that utilizes Gold coins, not representations of Gold coins. Historically, Gold has always operated alongside silver. Whether that would be the case in an era when Gold can be weighed in micrograms is moot. That will be up to the market to decide. A tradition going back to antiquity suggests that silver will be as popular and useful in the marketplace as it has always been.

Some people are sceptical of the idea of using Gold and silver coin as money, but as late as the 1960s many countries were still using silver coins. There was nothing startling or odd about it. A lack of familiarity with something does not mean that it lacks virtue. How could anything be more eccentric than believing that pieces of paper, redeemable for nothing whatsoever, are money?

Whether or not a Gold standard really is a Gold standard is determined by one factor—is Gold being used as the sole measure of value?

Any system that proposes that Gold be measured in terms of paper, or that Gold share the role of money with paper, or that Gold sit in a 'basket of commodities', is not the Gold standard. The idea that one can measure value with a piece of paper or a barrel of oil is akin to suggesting that one can measure the speed of sound with a turnip.

There are many, many different types of paper standards, but despite the pronouncements of various 'experts', the dictionary makes it quite clear and puts it well beyond debate, there is only one Gold standard. Either Gold is the measure and we have the Gold standard, or it is not the measure and we don't have the Gold standard. There is no comfortable space somewhere in between where politicians and central bankers can set up another self-serving, paper masquerade.

The classical Gold standard of the 19th century, the highest pinnacle of western society so far, was a quasi-Gold standard, but it was still better than everything that we have had since.

> ... the basic problem with all these gold standard systems was
> that they were all 'adulterated' ... i.e. they all had a fiduciary
> component.
>
> Rudy Fritsch

A 'fiduciary component' refers to a paper component that is not backed by Gold. 'Fiduciary' is derived from the Latin 'fidere'—to trust; in the case of paper, to trust governments and central bankers. Yes, there was a large Gold backing in the 19th century, but it was not the Gold standard because there was not enough Gold to back all the paper that was issued.

It was even worse when the UK tried to go back onto a 'Gold standard' in 1925. By then, there was even more un-backed paper in the system due to its expansion to finance the human catastrophe that was World War One. The 1925 U.K. 'Gold standard' was a mislabelled paper standard. It failed because the banknotes were redeemable for Gold in amounts of not less that a 400-ounce bar. Banknotes were only redeemable for the very rich.

Money was no longer for the people.

19ᵗʰ Century Prosperity

There is no attempt here to try to make the case that the classical 'Gold standard' produced instant prosperity for all, or that it was perfect. Poverty remained widespread, but judgement must be made on a relative basis. Prior to this era, the situation was very much worse. Rural life, subsequently idealised out of all recognition, was freely abandoned as people chose the prospects of jobs and opportunity offered by the city life. There can also be little doubt that prosperity would have spread even further and faster under the real Gold standard.

> Mere quotations of figures will not make clear the increased share of the national wealth which now finds its way into the pockets of the working classes, because of the unprecedented cheapness of all the necessaries and many of the luxuries of life (intoxicants alone excepted) has raised the buying power of wages in a degree which cannot be estimated.
>
> Sir Herbert Maxwell Bart MP 1897

Arthur Toynbee, the 19th century economic historian and social reformer, estimated that under the classical 'Gold standard' in the UK, by 1875 the working classes had amassed savings of £130,000,000. In light of the situation that existed just 100 years before, when most of these people had never seen a pound let alone owned one, this is an astonishing figure ... but only for those who do not comprehend the blessings of the accumulation and circulation of real money.

> ... in those thirty years (1851-1881) the wage-earning class had increased in number from 26,000,000 to 30,000,000 or 16 per cent; while the wages paid to them had increased by nearly 100 per cent. In fact the income of the working classes in 1881 was about equal to that of the whole nation in 1851, with largely increased purchasing power, owing to reduction in prices.
>
> W.H. Mallock, in an extensive analysis of British wages.

Not only were wages going up [**] whilst prices were falling, the hours worked to produce those increased wages were also falling. The concept

[**] Real wages doubled between 1860 and 1890—Brook and Watkins

of leisure time for working people first became a reality in the 19th century, as did the existence of a middleclass.

The accumulation and circulation of Gold began the process of removing the permanent wealth gap between the few born to luxury and the many born to abject poverty. The withdrawal of circulating Gold that was begun in 1914 ensured that not only was this process abruptly terminated, but that it was reversed.

From 1815 to 1914 the population of the UK increased almost 350%— from 10.25 million to over 46 million. This surge in population, at the same time as the general standard of living was rising, was unprecedented in history. By way of contrast, when Gold was withdrawn from the equation in 1914, the population growth dramatically slowed. In 2014, one hundred years later, the population is 64 million; an increase of only 36% and with a falling standard of living.

—⦇⦈—

It could be postulated that a true Gold standard would usher in an age such as would be talked about until the end of time. With all the impediments of the paper system that humanity labours under and is robbed by, still it has achieved miraculous advances. Modern technology coupled with money would transport humanity into a Golden age with benefits beyond current imagination. What peaks of society are available to humanity with the full mobilisation of Gold? As has been noted before, we can only clearly visualise what has been, not what has never been allowed to exist.

The Gold standard is defined:

> The use of money or its silver surrogate as the only measure of value.

—⦇⦈—

Gentlemen, in order to measure, you must define your unit.
British scientist Isaac Newton— Master of the (British) Mint

THE HOLY TRINITY OF MONEY

CHAPTER NINETEEN
THE HOLY TRINITY OF MONEY

Diamonds are forever

Shirley Bassey

Ms Bassey summed it up pithily, but why are diamonds forever? The importance of the stock-to-flow ratio of Gold and silver has become recognised over the last few years, but is there another commodity that has a high stock-to-flow ratio? An appreciation of this ratio and its importance to stability of value, must lead the questioning researcher to diamonds.

The word diamond is derived from the Greek adamas meaning invincible, unconquerable or indestructible. With its diamond ring symbolism of eternal and indestructible love, a diamond still remains faithful to those associations. Diamonds are made from carbon, which is the fundamental element of life on this planet.

Their discovery is first recorded in India, where they were brought to a sparkle at least 2,300 years ago. It was the cutting and polishing of diamonds to make religious icons that began the age-old and legendary Indian jewellery business*. Kautilya mentions diamonds in *The Arthahastra* dating from 296 BC. The detailed writings include the fact that there was

---

* It was also in BC India that the first industrial use of the smaller diamonds as drill bits was invented.

a superintendent charged with the examination of gems entering into the treasury; the same person was also the superintendent of Gold. There are no diamonds in their natural state in Egypt.

The exquisite beauty of diamonds, their ability to refract light and the discovery that they were 1000 times harder than the next hardest precious stones, rubies and sapphires, made them objects of wonder. Diamonds were, and still are, worn in women's nostrils in India with the aim (possibly optimistic) of enhancing sexual performance. They were reputed to have mysterious powers including healing and warding off enemies and evil forces.

Diamonds were accorded divine status and incorporated into Hindu religious ceremonies. The Greeks and Romans affirmed the belief of our ancients in a heavenly connection by describing diamonds as the teardrops of gods or the splinters of stars. Jewish high priests used diamonds to gauge innocence or guilt. A diamond held before an innocent person supposedly sparkled more brightly, whilst before a guilty person it dulled and darkened.

By the Middle Ages, the belief in the spiritual properties of diamonds had migrated to the Christian religion. It was believed that if a diamond were held in the hand while making the sign of the cross the person would be cured of illness. In 1532 Pope Clement VII ingested crushed diamonds in a bid to recover his failing health. It resulted in his death—most likely from his insides being cut to shreds. The fable that diamonds could bring about a cure by being ingested was followed by the fable that diamonds were poisonous. This came about because the spiritual and magical powers of diamonds started giving way to their commercial value. Mine owners did not want their workforce swallowing the diamonds in order to smuggle them out.

Up until the 14th century in western Europe it was decreed that only Kings could wear diamonds. They rode into battle wearing leather breastplates studded with them. The divine powers of the diamonds were believed to make them invincible. After the 14th century, they were worn more commonly, not so much as jewellery, but as an amulet that gave magical powers. They were also believed to impart virtue to the wearer.

Diamonds never achieved the divinity level of Gold or silver, in ancient times, as they did not have the status of representing the Sun or the Moon, the dominant heavenly bodies. However, the lesser process of deity identification did ensure that they became a good store of value, commensurate with that identification. It was the spiritual proximity of diamonds to the monetary metals that brought about their accumulation, the growing stock-to-flow ratio and their consequent relative stability of value over all time.

While diamonds are a weak link in the monetary chain, ranking well below Gold and silver, they hold their value more stably than anything except the monetary metals. It is primarily Gold, silver and diamonds that are secreted away in times of monetary debasement or the collapse of paper money. Most goods are subject to wild fluctuations in value under such circumstances.

Diamonds never made it as surrogate money because they didn't satisfy the requirements with the ease of silver. One large diamond is worth more than the sum of its divided parts. In terms of retained value, a diamond is only slightly more divisible than a goat; neither can be convincingly reassembled. Diamonds are neither fungible nor durable. They are extremely hard, yet if hit in the right place they will not only break, but shatter. These failures forever consigned diamonds to an ever diminishing spiritual relevance, 'a girl's best friend' (a pretty and relatively stable store of value) and industrial applications.

It is possible that the marketing of synthetic diamonds will damage their stability of value, though that has not happened to any great degree at this point. 'Synthetic' is misleading, because while they are synthetically produced, they are still real diamonds—crystallised carbon. The more appropriate name is considered to be 'laboratory grown'. Today, there is a vast stock of investment grade diamonds in the world. While it is beyond doubt that the ratio is high, neither stock nor flow can be accurately quantified. It seems reasonable to assume that the stock-to-flow ratio of diamonds is considerably larger than for other precious stones, if only on the basis of their relative durability and their former spiritual significance.

Diamonds retain an attenuated relationship with money that ensures their continued accumulation, and not only for the reason that their ornamental value far exceeds their industrial value. The special properties of diamonds are based on their ancient relationship with the divine metals and demonstrated by their ability to hold a fairly stable value.

Diamonds still hover aloof from mere precious stones and pearls[**] and remain something more than just another good. The faint memory of an illustrious past gives them a mysterious allure that harks back to a time when, but for a few physical properties, they could have attained the status of surrogate money.

---⁂---

Throughout the long history of our world, Gold, silver and diamonds have been the only three members of the Gold money family. Copper coins have circulated in many parts of the world, but copper was never money. As a 'bottom of the rung' coin they have been very successful, but only when in the exalted company of Gold and silver. The legitimacy of copper coins was based on the fact that they could be exchanged for the monetary metals. For example, in the U.K., twelve copper pennies could be exchanged for one silver shilling[***].

When divorced from Gold and silver and attached to paper money, the best that can be said for copper coins is that they always end up being

[**]   The pearls in the tomb of Tutankhamen found by Howard Carter crumbled to dust when touched. Pearls definitely do not have a large stock-to-flow ratio.

[***]   The copper coins were termed 'petty money', in contrast to the 'moneta grossa' (big money) as the Italians called the Gold and silver coins in the Renaissance period.

worth more than the paper ... no matter the size of the number printed on the paper. The coins do at least retain the value of their copper content. Copper's use in the hardening of Gold and silver coins in order to make them suitable for circulation, cannot be construed as implying any monetary properties to copper.

Despite the fact that diamonds have no monetary role to play in today's world, they are of interest to a fuller understanding of the story of money.

Gold emerged triumphant as money because of its identification with the Sun God. It was Gold, and only Gold, that was, is, and will always be, the store of stable value. However, it remains important to recognize the pedigree of silver and diamonds as demonstrated by their relatively stable values. They still carry a mystique and importance that soars serenely above their value as pretty and useful goods.

Gold, silver and diamonds are the holy trinity of money and all will carry the importance and stature of that within the consciousness of humanity until the dusk of time.

CHAPTER TWENTY
ANOTHER MONEY

*Ex scientia pecuniae libertas—Out of knowledge of money
comes freedom*

The search for Gold's mysterious origins touched upon many disciplines. A question arose: has there ever been another legitimate money? Has there ever been another commodity with stable value?

Not only did another money exist, its shadow still lingers in the English language. 'To shell out', still carries the meaning of handing over money for something. Cowry (also Cowrie) shells have been widely noted as legitimate money. They were a separate development from Gold, though from the same contra intuitive source. The similarities to Gold are so remarkable that it would be neglecting the real story of money to not touch upon them.

Cowry shells have circulated more widely than any coin, even the ubiquitous Roman coin. They originated from the Indo-Pacific region, but were mostly from the Maldives where their collection and cleaning was industrialised. The Maldives became the lucrative centre for the world trade in Cypraea Moneta—Cowry money[*]. Cowry shells were used in northern Australia, Asia (including China, India and Thailand), Africa and parts

---

[*]   Cypraea Annulus was also used. It is visually very similar to Moneta; it is slightly darker and has a yellow ring around the dorsal area.

of Europe. They even made their way across the ocean to pre-Columbus North America, but there is no evidence of them having been used in commercial exchange there.

Cowry shells were used from Palaeolithic times, right up to the 20th century. In the same manner as Gold, the cowry shell became a spiritual representation that was hoarded long before its marketplace application was discovered.

Prior to the Gold of the Sun God, much of the world lived in matriarchal societies. This is evidenced by the Mother Figures that are still being dug up. Mostly they are distortions of the female body with grotesquely exaggerated hips and vulva. This was because they were co-representations of both the female figure and the cowry shell, which has a vulva shaped opening. The Mother Figure was recognised as the source of life and revered. Cowry shells were religious icons[**].

Because of the miraculous powers of Gold in the marketplace (post 1500 BC), the Sun God became the dominant deity and became associated with the source of all life. Gradually the use of cowry as money died out, though remnants of it still exist in remote areas of Africa in the 21st century. Unlike Gold, they were volitionally abandoned, not forced out of the markets by governments.

Is Cowry the Exception to the Golden Rule?

At first glance, cowry does appear a to be the exception to the Golden rule. Its easy alignment with Gold's origin and marketplace roles is of enormous interest. It also points us in the direction of something that is intriguing. Surely it cannot be put down to mere coincidence that in this planet's long history, spanning hundreds of millennia, that the only stores of stable value to have surfaced (literally) both arrived from a spiritual source? It seems

---

[**]   Cowry also had other representations, particularly in Africa where it came to symbolise the 'evil eye'.

to confirm that money can only be gained from the opposite end of the stability of value spectrum from goods. This is an easy logic to follow: the marketplace is the arena of the greatest instability of value and would be a most unlikely source of the stable value necessary for money.

That cowry was money has further support from the fact that it had a reasonably high stock-to-flow ratio and it was impossible to counterfeit. Its failure to perform many of the other requirements of money in the modern sense however meant that its use dwindled over the centuries.

The Almost Money

Reports state that the value of cowry increased the further that it travelled from its Indo-Pacific sources. Circa 850 AD, Arab traders are recorded as purchasing one million cowry shells for one Gold dinar in the Maldives, then selling them in one thousand lots for one Gold dinar in Nigeria. While attention is drawn to the outstanding profit, the more important point to note is that cowries were being measured in Gold; therefore cowries were, at least by this time, a good, not money.

The fact that cowry shells eventually disappeared from the marketplace in the presence of Gold also indicates that they were not real money. Had they been a store of stable value then a permanent ratio of value between cowry and Gold would have eventuated and they would have continued to circulate in tandem. The value of the cowrie seems to have fluctuated based on supply and demand. That is a quality of a good, not money. Whilst that differentiates it from Gold, the fact that cowry continued to perform its monetary role alongside Gold for a while in some areas of Africa, China and India highlights a remarkable similarity to silver.

On the other hand, maybe cowries were genuine money but, lacking the durability and divisibility of Gold and silver and some other attributes, they gave way as the market expressed its preference (the most marketable money?).

Gold's superior lineage, coupled with its greater efficacy in the marketplace, broke the agreement that shells were a store of stable value. Cowries returned to their status as a good. The process of deterioration from a store of stable value to a good likely happened very gradually—over centuries. The invention of the wireless telegraph, allowing fast, long distance communication, would have speeded up the process. The knowledge that cowry's value was perceived differently in different places would have detracted from its credibility as money.

What stops cowry from being dismissed as just another trade good is the fact that they were not a typical trade good. Other than as ornaments they had no practical use. Before cowry became used in the marketplace, its main value was as a symbol—a symbol of the divine Matriarch. Judging by the precedent of Gold, it was the stock-to-flow ratio derived from this that led to the cowry's application in the marketplace. It is this not inconsiderable similarity, which gives valid ground for comparing cowry with Gold. Its parallel use as money alongside Gold is also unique.

> They called them (cowries) Boly and export to all parts an infinite quantity, in such wise that in one year I have seen 30 or 40 whole ships loaded with them without other cargo. All go to Bengal for there only is there a demand for a large quantity at high prices. The people of Bengal use them for ordinary money although they have gold and silver and plenty of other metals; and what is more strange, kings and great lords have houses built expressly to store these shells and treat them as part of their treasure.
>
> Pyrard de Laval—he was wrecked on the Maldives in the 17th century and lived there for two years.

Weighing all factors in the balance, it is hard to concur with the prevailing wisdom that cowrie was ever money in the total sense that Gold is money, but it would be too casual to dismiss the possibility. At the least, they were a unique 'almost money' and worthy of a closer examination than is given here. Even diamonds, with the advantage of their special relationship with Gold, did not have the profound impact of cowry shells.

Another Money—Part Two

Could another money come into existence? It is certainly possible to postulate a larger stock-to-flow ratio. Consider the situation of a new metal that is discovered somewhere and 500,000 tonnes is dug out of the ground. Then it is discovered that other sources of this metal are miniscule, to the degree that if every one of these other source was mined extensively, then it would only produce 1000 tonnes a year. Overnight we would have a commodity with a stock-to-flow ratio greater than gold.

Would it be acceptable as money, and if not why not?

Speculation strongly suggests that even in this wildly improbable scenario the new metal would be still valued in terms of gold. Why? Because gold was the first store of stable value. The millennia long, worldwide and culturally indifferent agreement that gold is money is the ultimate determinant. Which would you accept for your good: Gold with its millennia long proven stability of value, or Metal X with its theoretical stability of value?

A new unit of measure of liquid volume or weight could be inflicted by government legislation; no such option exists with the measure of value. Humanity's history teaches many lessons for those prepared to heed them; it certainly informs us that Gold and only Gold is money and that government legislation, no matter how harsh the enforcement, is ultimately impotent in this unique area.

———∞———

The untold story of money shows Gold's influence consistently at the centre of human achievement. One facet has only been hinted at to this point. Does Gold have an historical importance that exceeds even that of its monetary derivative?

From the different cultures and religions of the world comes affirmation of just that.

Chapter Twenty-one
In the Beginning

Astronomy compels the soul to look upward, and leads us from this world to another.

Plato

The miracle that money brought about was not performed in isolation; there was one other pertinent factor in humanity's transition from huddling under trees and in caves to lounging in air-conditioned condos.

This final piece of the puzzle further explains the significance of the Sun God, which in turn further fleshes out the background to Gold's stability of value. It does not much improve the understanding of money, and in that respect could have been omitted, but it does allow a better understanding of the peerless influence of Gold on human development ...

———⊗⊗⊗———

The night sky no longer holds the fascination of old. Neon signs, streetlights, pollution and roofed dwellings mean that the stars are almost invisible. Along with the passing of the age of the sky have gone romantic poems and songs about love under the silvery moon. But more, the popular questioning of the nature of man's role in the universe, a general sense of intellectual probing and wonder, has become weakened to the point of disappearing. It has been replaced by the ascendance of the mundane and trivial, from stargazing to pop stargazing and star signs. Questions have become smaller, much smaller—lives also.

By contrast, the undimmed, twinkling night sky of our ancestors spectacularly commanded attention; starlight fanned the embers of the soul and ignited intellectual fires.

Prehistoric rock art displayed charts of the skies. A handful of these first astronomers, staring in awe at the nightly display, made a connection between two wondrous phenomena. One, as previously noted, was that the properties of the Sun aligned perfectly with the yellow metal that they came across while hunting and gathering. The other was of momentous significance; it was that there was a cyclic continuity to the movement of the heavenly bodies; their motions were predictable. It is not at all certain that the first phenomenon would have amounted to anything without the appreciation of its relevance to the second.

From this connection stemmed the whole intellectual paradigm of human thought that reached its apex in the 19th century.

It was no coincidence that the first great tribes were those that had begun to chart the heavens; it was only this that allowed the subsequent insights. Though Gold was still millennia away from being money, its connection with the Sun now impacted on human thought with the subtlety of a meteor strike.

Human's hunted and gathered by day and huddled for safety around campfires at night. Out of the dark came unknown sounds and movements. While life on Earth seemed in a constant state of chaotic and frightening change, the heavenly bodies to which their Gold provided humanity a direct link displayed an ordered and rhythmic predictability. The contrast was stark; the possibilities profound.

What the earliest astronomers gained from their perception of the yellow metal's connection to the Sun was a sense that life was a cycle and that through their Gold they were a part of that cycle. Humanity was as one with a vast and mysterious universal continuity. Unknown millennia later this sense of a connection between Gold and the grand cosmos still meanders around the periphery of human consciousness.

Gold presented humanity with the understanding that life was a progression—not only from day to day and from year to year, but also from generation to generation and, maybe, from lifetime to lifetime. The Sun God was the first cosmic deification[*]. This marked the precise beginning of Gold accumulation—holy Gold. The early astronomers morphed into the priesthood, the observatories became temples, and humanity set off in a grand new direction.

The impact of Gold changed the world forever—long before it became money.

⸺⧼⧽⸺

The Gold Portal

Then felt I like some watcher of the skies
When a new planet swims into his ken.

John Keats

Through the Gold portal that led to the Sun God, humanity entered a new plane of existence. It was the beginning of contemplation; of concepts that were formed above and beyond those forged in the struggle for immediate survival. It was not only the birth of the universal god—monotheism; it was the birth of the intellectual—the philosopher. Though the world was still tribal, here was the spark, not so much of understanding, but of the need for understanding. It was the beginning of the search for ultimate truth. The philosophical history

---

[*]   Evidence, particularly from the 'Old Europe' as painstakingly constructed by Marija Gimbutas, points to the cyclical nature of the seasons having formed the belief in an Earth bound goddess—possibly prior to the emergence of the Sun God. If there was a prior Moon goddess, could there be a connection between her usurpation by the universal male Sun God and the world changing from matriarchal to patriarchal societies?

of at least the last 9,000 years has consisted of the exploration of humanity's link with the heavens.

There have been as many theories as there have been philosophers.

———— ⣀ ————

The concept of a cyclic continuity pushed human thought toward the future. Gold lifted humanity out of its drudgery by creating a sense of what could be, rather than just what was and what had been.

The present is a vantage point from which one can look either backwards or forwards. This is evident at the level of individuals and groups. Some have a gaze fixated on the past; others are more inclined to the future. As those who look to the future for solutions are inclined to innovation and entrepreneurialism, so those who look to the past are inclined to stagnation and academia.

By providing a sense of continuity, Gold encouraged humanity to look to a point beyond their next meal. It encouraged them to plan and hope and dream. A gaze fixated on the past does not allow for hopes and dreams. Such people are in dull acceptance of the present, or if they have a vague sense that the situation could be improved, search for a remedy in the past.

The lives of those who tread the path of daily survival are made bearable to the same degree that they are able to confidently project that survival into the future. The more future that can be projected, the more tolerable becomes the present. It is only by means of the ability to create the future that day-to-day lives are given meaning. Gold, in its unique role as the store of stable value, has been and remains, the most significant instrument in allowing people to shape the future and by doing so live happily in the present.

———— ⣀ ————

From the tribal beginnings to the peak of society, Gold and humanity have been and remain inextricably linked. Initially by the more sophisticated, future-orientated thinking that flowed from the observed connection between Gold and the Sun God, then by the utilization of money to facilitate complex exchange and accumulations.

The story of Gold is the story of human achievement. It explains much that has seemed obscure, including why tribes rise to the status of society and then fall back again. It is only by a clearer knowledge of the mechanism that has brought humanity to this point that we can ensure future progress. Without that clarity it would be easy to lose everything.

A store of stable value, which had validity everywhere and at all times, eventually found its way to its rightful throne at the centre of commerce. This was the second coming of Gold that is the theme of this book. It was the emergence of Gold as money that allowed for trade on a grand scale. It was the exponential growth in trade that allowed the tribes to develop into the great societies.

The journey from late New Kingdom Egypt to the present has not always been smooth, but generally speaking it has been one of incremental progress spread over 3,500 years. Reversion from such a great height would not be in the same manner. Falling is faster than climbing; collapsing is faster than building.

> It would be some consolation for the feebleness of our selves and our works if all things should perish as slowly as they come into being; but as it is, increases are of sluggish growth, but the way to ruin is rapid.
>
> Lucius Anneaus Seneca

Money has been the most misunderstood of subjects. Even sex, with all its troubles, seems like a calm body of transparent water by comparison. For hundreds of thousands, maybe millions, of years there was zero human progress. Human progress was not automatic; it needed a catalyst; that catalyst was Gold. It still is. To survive, societies need Gold and silver just as surely as the human body needs air and water.

Humanity will again come to view the stars as a part of their existence, and questions and lives revert to more importance in consequence. Even wrong answers are superior to no questions.

Gold's early encouragement to explore the concept of the future produced results that would have been far beyond the ability of our forebears to imagine. Similarly today, the freeing up of Gold to perform its natural roles to the fullest extent possible would produce wondrous changes that are beyond our imagination. The world has rarely witnessed the free and unfettered use of Gold. Those times were too brief and the records too sparse to provide reliable enlightenment.

It cannot be definitively stated that the result would be prosperity beyond imagination. There was though a progression from the widespread poverty of the world, to a surge in prosperity when money began to circulate and accumulate. Is it not reasonable then to postulate that an even greater prosperity would come about with an unfettered and unrestrained circulation and accumulation of Gold?

It is arrogance or a lack of imagination to believe that the world has already witnessed the peak of civilisation; to assume that the ideal would be a return to the past, to such periods as the classical 'Gold standard'. The world is improved by advancing, not by regressing. A regression would, at best, lead the world right back to where it is now. Surely humanity can strive for better than that?

Gold impels humanity toward the future, not the past; it has done so since the first astronomers travelled through the Gold portal all those millennia ago.

So is Gold perfect as money? The answer has to be 'no'. Perfection no more exists in money than it does in people—or books.

CHAPTER TWENTY-TWO
GOLD'S ACHILLES HEEL

*The gold standard sooner or later will return with the
force and inevitability of natural law, for it is the money of
freedom and honesty.*

Hans F. Sennholz

As already noted, Gold's value in the marketplace is too high for practical purposes, but there is another flaw in this most noble of metals and it is one that silver cannot compensate for. Gold is one of the most durable metals known. Its lack of corrosion is famous, as is evidenced by the fact that items of Gold have been recovered from millennia past in perfect condition. Age does not noticeably weary Gold, however the constant jingling, rubbing, passing and dropping associated with the marketplace does. The addition of small amounts of copper does not remove this problem; it only reduces the severity.

In this single manner, while Gold and silver are the most practical metals available for coinage, they are not perfect. We should not dwell on or highlight this weakness, rather we should marvel at how perfect and irreplaceable are the monetary metals in every other respect. Nevertheless, this weakness must be acknowledged and addressed. It is surprising that those who attack Gold never bring up this solitary legitimate weakness of the monetary metals. All other objections can be blown away with a featherweight of logic, but this problem is genuine. Any discussion on the use of Gold as the circulating money in the 21st century must take into account this factor. In the 19th century, Gold coins were returned to the mint on average every 18 years due to wear. Silver, being the coin used in the marketplace, was returned more frequently.

Modern technology allows for coins to be embedded in an embossed, durable and secure plastic coating. Alternatively, precise weights of Gold or silver could be inserted into the centre of copper coins. These technologies, or something similar, need to be developed, perfected and implemented prior to any circulation. The most credible and acceptable coins will be those that have surmounted the wear factor. Not only is the wear of coins in the modern day an unnecessary waste, for surely that fine dust is not recoverable, but it also leads to another more severe problem.

— ∞ —

The Primary Reason for Coin Adulteration

In 14th century England the wear of coins was used as the justification for adulterating later issues. The reasoning, borne from experience, was that if a percentage of each coin in circulation had been lost to wear, then to put out new coins with a full weight would see the new coins disappear into hoards. Why would people part with the new full-weight coin if they could dump the old low-weight one? During the reign of Richard II, the loss due to wear of silver coins after 30 years of circulation was put at about 20%[*]. This was exacerbated by the lack of milled edges leading to deliberate shaving, but the loss from genuine wear would still have been significant.

The curiosity is that this is only a problem for the Gold standard, not the 19th century quasi Gold standard. Under the latter, people accepted that

---

[*]   Introduction by Charles Johnston to *De Moneta* by Nicole Oresme. In the modern world it would be a far higher percentage after 30 years because of the increased velocity of circulation.

banknotes were as good as Gold. They were, after all, believed to be redeemable for Gold. That being the case, no matter how worn the coin, it could always be exchanged for banknotes that were accepted by almost everyone.

Under the Gold standard this will not be the case. The most worn coins will be exchanged in the market before all others because not all coins will be regarded as equal; for in truth they will not be. The newer issues will be of the stated weight; the old coins will have fallen below their stated weight. In effect this means that new coins will fail to circulate except in extremis. An increase in the coin supply will not lead to the same increase of coins in circulation. Many of the new coins will disappear into hoards.

Simultaneously, the market would discount the worn coins and give preference to the new coins. This would be a far from ideal situation that to a degree would 'gum up' the market. The whole virtue and purpose of Gold coin is the certainty of weight and fineness—'a known value'. Without this the marketplace would, to a degree, return to the period of 1500 BC to 650 BC. During this time, Gold was used as money, but every trade was encumbered by the need to check the weight and fineness of the money. It was only when the people of Lydia produced the first coins of a set weight and fineness circa 650 BC that trade became easier and faster and the transition to the modern world was completed.

This problem of wear has been used as the justification for adulteration since the monetary metals were first coined. Coin wear encouraged the minting of new coins that did not conform to the original weight, but to the weight of the average coin already in circulation. It was an attempt to ensure that the new coins circulated. While understandable, it is easy to see where this path leads; ultimately the coins are adulterated to worthlessness. The problem was very real and the solution in previous centuries was not obvious, barring a prohibitively expensive full recall of all prior coins with the cost borne by the bearer. This would have been considered less politically feasible than adulteration.

The problem was not restricted to natural wear and clipping. Putting coins into a bag and jingling them (known as sweating) for hours and hours would produce metallic dust at the bottom of the bag. More extreme methods included drilling a hole through the middle of the coin and then hammering the coin inwards to fill it up again.

In the 21st century the solution to all these problems is more readily available to us. Coin damage, of one sort or another, is a problem that needs to be solved.

CHAPTER TWENTY-THREE
GOLD AND DEMOCRACY

Everyone wants to live at the expense of the state.
They forget that the state lives at the expense of everyone.

Frederic Bastiat

The irredeemable paper money of the modern era was put in place in 1914[*]. To the average person, the government seemed to have suddenly moved into the business of wealth creation, to be somehow creating its own money. Without the necessity to back the paper with Gold, ever-greater amounts were printed and ever-greater debt taken on to pay for ever-more promises. Prudent objections were ignored; few bothered to inspect the long-term effects of such profligate behaviour.

Since time immemorial, it had been easily understood that governments lived at the expense of the people. In the 20th century, this became supplanted by the notion that people lived off governments. Our political leaders solemnly intoned messages about bringing prosperity to the nation; very few had the wit to laugh at these naked emperors. It was by the process of endless borrowing that governments were able to create and nurture this illusion.

In the guise of short-term prosperity, they brought long-term ruin.

---

[*]   In Europe and the British Empire, 1933 in the US

Business and wealth creation was relegated to something that was of questionable morality and that existed courtesy of the government—for as long as it stayed within tolerable bounds. In prior ages, the brightest and most able became the hunters of the tribe. When they returned with their wealth, the dead deer and pigs, they were feted as heroes. They were recognised as the backbone of society.

Since the dawn of the agricultural era, it is the entrepreneur who has filled the same role. Today, far from being feted as heroes, they are relegated to the status of social pariah. Wealth creation is regarded with suspicion and even distaste; something that the government must regulate lest it get out of control. Common sense has departed the area. Wealth creation is no longer perceived as being necessary for survival, a social blessing, or even validated as the result of successful prediction, risk and hard work. There is a vague sense that widespread prosperity is a product of governments and exists despite the exploitations of businesses.

Over time, and with governments established as self-financing entities, a majority of people came to vote for the politicians and political parties that promised to spend the most. What they received back from governments of course was never even close to compensating them for what they had lost via taxation—present and future. In a farcical pantomime, the more people lost, the louder became their demands for governments to spend more, tax more and degrade the paper further.

The principal victims of this are usually its most ardent supporters.

The demands, vote-buying schemes and consequent debts grew ever more fanciful. The 20th century became the century of the free lunch; all those so inclined were invited to live off the State. This orgy of monetary promiscuity reached a peak when governments began to borrow money to send overseas in the form of aid to less enlightened countries. The illusion was shattered by the reality of government debts that became so gigantic that even the interest became un-payable, never mind the principal.

The market, belatedly noticing this phenomenon, became reluctant to buy government bonds.

The Age of Default began.

How did this bizarre Alice-in-Wonderland situation come to pass? It was not only the direct result of abandoning the use of Gold as money—it was the reason for doing so. The sole purpose for governments discontinuing the circulation of Gold was to print more bank notes to pay for debts—originally war debts. People had come to trust banknotes so much that they had forgotten that they could be only as good as the Gold that backed them.

The belief that paper money can operate in the same manner as money is up there with the belief that the world is flat. That there still exists in the 21ˢᵗ century a Flat Earth Society is not cause for optimism that the idea of paper money will finally be consigned to history's rubbish bin for failed experiments. It is likely that devotees of the Flat Money Society will be around for a while yet.

Death by Voting

Governments cannot print Gold; while this is a common statement, the implications are not well understood. When Gold was in use during the 19ᵗʰ century, people understood very clearly that all government expenditure could only come from the pockets of taxpayers. For that reason, people were inclined to vote for the politicians who promised to spend the least. Conversely, under the system of paper money where governments appear to be self-financing entities, voters are inclined to support the politicians who promise to spend the most. It is a profound difference.

It became apparent many decades ago that democracy could not survive without a return to honest money.

This should not be taken to mean that during periods when Gold was in use all governments lived within their means. Governments always attempt to spend more than they have; it is their modus operandi. The classical Gold standard did not prohibit borrowings, but it did restrain them to manageable levels. It is for this reason that Gold is always eventually withdrawn from circulation by governments—always. Even with all the Gold and silver flowing into Spain during the pillage of Las Indias, the recklessly extravagant spending on wars meant that the Spanish government still could not pay its bills. Their debts were repudiated in 1557, 1575, 1596, 1607, 1627 and 1647[**]. They make the recent Argentine governments look positively prudent.

People are beginning to wake up to the fact that it is they who are paying, not only for the welfare handouts, but also the sovereign debts and future obligations that their governments have run up. They still do not understand the process, but they can feel and see the result. This modicum of clarity is arriving too late. The debts are now so vast that they can never be repaid in real value, but even that is not the worst of the problem.

Paper money is brought into existence by borrowing—by debt; by its nature it cannot pay off that same debt without creating more debt.

———— ✸ ————

Global Credit Crisis

And so the reality is beginning to penetrate the deep fog of public discourse that this is not a Global Financial Crisis, always a red herring, it is, and always has been, a Global Credit Crisis. The world's credit system, paper backed only by debt, is imploding. The inherent instability of paper money has caused a resonance throughout the whole economy. The further that instability projects and the longer it occurs, the worse the instability becomes. It has changed nothing with the policies of our governments; they

---

[**]   *The Age of Reason Begins 1961*—Will and Ariel Durant

have continued to follow the same course. The truth is that they cannot stop; the structure of the paper money system dictates that any cessation of borrowing will cause the system to implode.

> Our monetary system is lurching from crisis to crisis, on its way to collapse. Debt is growing out of control, rising at an exponential rate. It's not merely that Congress lacks discipline. The problem is that the dollar is irredeemable. It's an IOU. An IOU cannot extinguish a debt, only shift it. The interest can't be paid off either, so it accumulates. Every year, the debt grows by at least the accrued interest.
>
> Keith Weiner,
> President of the Gold Standard Institute—US

Not a single country has reduced its debt; at best they have reduced the amounts that they are continuing to borrow. In other words, sovereign debt all over the world is continuing to expand. Even this is not because of any surge in responsibility, but because they cannot borrow what they would like, and because they dare not stop. The debt is a cancer that is killing its host.

At five minutes to the midnight of the most calamitous monetary collapse in the history of the world, we have not even reached the point of seriously talking about beginning a transition to real money. The Age of Default has further to progress before rational discussions begin. The fantasy of a paper money system that can be digitally created remains too alluring. Politicians are quite unable, both morally and intellectually, to consider the ramifications of what they have inflicted on societies.

The regime of paper money has undermined the viability of the middleclass, banks, pension funds, insurance companies and governments. It has also produced a situation that will bring into doubt the credibility of democracy itself. Let it be understood that the blame lies not with democracy, but with the false incentives of paper money. A wrong incentive will always produce a wrong result.

Chapter Twenty-four
Of Coins and Kings

Weight and measure are the first things to prove, for all is
chaos where there is deceit in the unit of measurement.

Cassiodorus 5th century BC

What is the reason for the millennia long track record of the heads of royals and presidents appearing on coins? It is unlikely that it was to identify the origin of the coin as suggested by Nicole Oresme[*]. If the origin of the coin were deemed important, rather than its weight and fineness, then the more logical representation would have been the local produce—corn, wheat, cows, wine or weapons etc. These would also have been far easier to depict than a recognisable face. The crude minting methods that existed for the early coins, basically form and hammer, would have made facial recognition very difficult.

The original Lydian coin (circa 650 BC) showed the shining Sun behind the lion's head; the Sun also featured on other early coins[**]. Gold and silver were still recognised as having religious significance and it was represented

---

[*]   *De Moneta*

[**]   This lends limited support to the speculation that the original coins were designed as temple tokens. Amusingly, this obvious sun has been described as 'possibly a wart' on the lion's nose.

in the coin. By 200 BC, the religious icons had largely disappeared, to be replaced by the face of the ruler of the day. It can be reasonably assumed that the depiction was designed to associate the ruler with godly powers. Marketing has been around for a long while. This warped into the idea that the money was the responsibility of the monarch. This was an assumed claim with no legitimacy other than self-interest.

The overwhelming dominance and familiarity of money in the marketplace began to obscure the reason for Gold's stability of value. Eventually the significance of Gold became lost in the mists of time. All that remains in the present is the blurred half-thought in the more perceptive that there is more to Gold than meets the eye.

Money was not an invention of kings or emperors or anyone else; it was the representation of humanity's intellectual striving and spiritual awakening—a gift of the Sun God if you will. Money was born of the people and forever belongs to the people. Control of the money supply means, to some degree or other, control of every single exchange of goods. For over 2,500 years this monopoly control has been abused to the point where money was reliably adulterated to the point of worthlessness.

From Aristotle in the 4th century BC, to Oresme in the 14th century AD, a period of 1,800 years, it was argued that money belonged to the people, not to the State. After that, State ownership became accepted as a *fait accompli*, mostly by virtue of the fact that private minting was punished by the separation of head from torso. This usurpation of the people's money by their rulers, circa 560 BC, is the source of Knapp's claim that money was an invention of governments.

It was not money that governments invented; it was the monopolising of money.

Today, very few understand the pernicious fraud of a State that first assumes a monopoly of the money, and then abolishes it by instating adulterated coin or paper in its place. Money belongs to the people who created it, and who own and exchange with it. The most dangerously corrupting power of governments is their claimed right to a monopoly control of not only the money supply, but of what is used as money. This first step on the road to tyranny is the foundation for many (all?) other government excesses. No real reformation of government, and surely this is needed, can begin until money returns to the people from whom it was expropriated.

The freedom to mine, refine, hold, hoard, save, mint, exchange, invest, and transport Gold, unimpeded at any step of the way by the state, is the most fundamental requirement of a free society. All other rights and freedoms can only exist with these freedoms intact.

With government control of money, the public has no recourse to punish those who destroy their wealth. The reputation of a private company and its directors would be irrevocably harmed if a single coin was found to be in any way adulterated or below weight. A free market in money is the ultimate empowerment of the people.

Off with the heads of kings and presidents, and on with the logos of private companies.

Separation of Money and State

As the separation of Church and State marked one of the finest achievements of western society, so the return to a separation of Money and State will mark the beginning of humanity's renaissance.

Only circulating Gold can assure the supremacy of human nature over government nature. The size of the economy and its globalised nature makes doubly dangerous and destructive any artificial concentration of monetary power. Humanity has a stark choice: either the Gold standard with liberty, prosperity and peace, or government monopoly of the money supply with grinding poverty or worse for all except the well connected.

In the entire course of human history, not one government has ever managed a nation's money over the longer term in such a way that it benefited the people. Since 560 BC, governments have first seized control of money and then degraded it. Eventually they destroy the wealth of the nation. Whenever control of the money supply has become centralised it has ended in disaster. History's lesson is quite clear: no governing body, of any political persuasion, can long keep from debasing the coin (adulterating Gold or silver with base metals), or even more cynically, replacing it with pieces of paper. Money is far too important to be left in the hands of governments.

As it is undeniable that people should be free to choose the goods that they do or do not wish to purchase, so it is equally valid that they be allowed the freedom to use the money of their choice. A situation where people voluntarily exchange will always be not just more efficient, but more moral. There is every reason to believe that under such a scenario people would again choose Gold and silver.

⎯⎯∞⎯⎯

The only thing that stops humanity from achieving unimaginable levels of prosperity, and innovating its way throughout the Solar System and beyond, is control of the money supply by governments. Eventually, as with the straw and the camel, the ever-greater debasement of money breaks the back of society and it collapses. It is not hard to understand. The fall of societies is not part of any mystical or natural cycle; it is the consequence of allowing governments the monopoly right to adulterate or synthesize money.

The history of modern societies, exemplified by, but not limited to, the Roman, Chinese, British and American, shows clearly that they rise through the ingenuity and productivity of their people, and then fall through the destructive monetary policies of their governments.

⎯⎯∞⎯⎯

Floating Paper Monies

Today the world uses 'floating' paper monies. This means that market forces determine their value. Speculators buy and sell them, just like they buy and sell pork bellies or wheat. On the surface, and it is defended as such, this is encouraging the actions of the free market. In truth it is the opposite; more damning, it is the tacit admission that the whole system of paper money is once again failing.

Money must be the measure of value. How can the measure, any measure, be subject to transient market forces? Can a wheat merchant say that a tonne means this weight one day and a lesser or greater weight the next? Of course not, that would lead to utter pandemonium in the wheat markets. Trading would grind to a halt until the mess had been sorted out. The measure must be stable, otherwise it is not a measure and markets would eventually cease to function. To stress this is not radical; that the measure must be sacrosanct has been accepted for many thousands of years.

> I have not increased nor diminished the measure, I have not diminished the palm; I have not encroached upon the fields.
> I have not added to the balance weights; I have not tampered with the plumb bob of the balance.
> To be sworn before god

> From Chapter 125 of the *Egyptian Book of the Dead*

The measure cannot be subject to arbitrary whim. Paper monies are insidiously destroying markets. Their 'floating' by governments is the acknowledgement that what is being used for money is not a stable value and therefore cannot be the measure of value. For that reason, trade will continue to diminish until either money is allowed to perform its legitimate roles, or trade—national and international—collapses.

The most famous paper money collapse of modern times [***] was the Weimar Republic collapse of 1923. Severe though that was, its effects were eased by the

---

[***]   The worst was the Hungarian monetary collapse of 1945—1946.

relative health of many of the surrounding countries. Goods still flowed into the country, with Gold and silver, and paper monies from all over Europe, being utilized instead of wheelbarrow loads of Reich Marks. What happens when all the interlinked paper monies of the world collapse together?

To those who wish to wield power over the lives of others, the temptation to seize control of the money supply is irresistible. That control has an attendant history of war and impoverishment going back millennia. Money should no more be under the control of a central authority than should any other item involved in a trade. When government controls the supply of toilet paper, then we know at once that the toilet paper will be of low quality, highly priced and in short supply[****]. This only interferes negatively in one area though ... toilet paper. With government control of money and credit, the consequences are spread catastrophically throughout the whole economy. Not a single trade can occur that is untainted by the distortions of government control.

> As destructive as government interference is in the area of production, it is that much worse in the area of money and credit. Every aspect of production and trade depends on money, so distortions in this area are magnified.
>
> Keith Weiner

The explosion of prosperity in the 19th century, by the simple expedient of allowing the circulation of money, paralleled the situation in Egypt circa 1500 BC when Gold first entered the marketplace. All that is necessary for people to achieve prosperity is for the marketplace to have access to real money. Conversely, a situation of widespread and sustained poverty can only be brought about by the denial of the same. Prosperity has nothing to do with whether or not a country is endowed with natural resources. The only resource necessary for prosperity is a free people able to access and utilize money unhindered by government regulations.

[****]   Oddly enough, at the very time of writing this, it is reported that the Venezuelan government has taken over the manufacture and supply of toilet paper with the predicted results.

Societies rise through the utilisation of Gold and silver in the marketplace. Then, after governments first assume a monopoly of the money supply and then, invariably and inevitably degrade that money, they fall. As the money fails so does society. Such is the uncomplicated lesson from the whole of recorded history.

CHAPTER TWENTY-FIVE

CRISIS

*It is not the cost of returning to gold circulation that is
astronomical, but the cost of not returning.*

Professor Antal E. Fekete

Claude Henri de Rouvroy, Comte de Saint-Simon (1760–1825) was a
French aristocrat. He observed and wrote about the emergence of the
industrial revolution with its new industries and the consequent rising
prosperity of working people. Saint-Simon seems to have been the first to
note that this was a new structure for doing business. The owners sat at the
top of a pyramid; underneath were shareholders, then beneath them were
managers and at the bottom were the workers who produced the goods.

Saint-Simon realised that this new paradigm designed for mass
production was the secret to a powerful new way of producing goods and
prosperity. He developed theories on how this structure could be improved,
including the proposal that scientists should sit at the top of the pyramid.
Saint-Simon died in penniless obscurity. Unfortunately, his ideas lived on,
though in altered form.

Karl Marx was deeply impressed and influenced by Saint-Simon's
writings. He proposed his own variation on the theory. The State would
assume control of the top of the structure and then the workers could receive

the profits. Marx perceived the entrepreneurial owners and shareholders as parasites. The State would abolish property rights, confiscate the means of production and run it all with a central administration.

Marx was the ultimate reactionary—history's great counterrevolutionary. What he proposed in *Das Kapital* was nothing short of a return to pre 1500 BC—to a goldless economy centrally planned by a ruling elite with institutionalised poverty for the masses. The whole world is currently bogged in the unfolding of this dystopia. The millennia long, market-driven, Gold-powered process of freeing people from bondage and poverty has been reversed. State run education is failing, home ownership is once again moving beyond the grasp of working people, jobs are disappearing and funding for the arts and charities is in precipitous decline. Judged by any yardstick the standard of living for the average person is falling.

Marx overlooked or underestimated three crucial factors. His first and most egregious error was ignoring the entire history of exchange and Gold and the consequent growth of the world's great societies. By this one oversight his theories were reduced to Mills & Boon economics—full of wishful thinking and romantic notions largely divorced from reality.

The second was the drive and skill of the entrepreneur and investors in developing a business concept and turning it into a successful enterprise. This included the risk factor; an enterprise could only flourish and make a profit if the product was in complete accord with what the consumer wanted and could afford. It was and remains a much-overlooked fact that for a business, the opposite of profit is loss—loss of capital and loss of jobs.

Whenever a profit is gained, a loss was risked.

Only someone who has invested money, time and ideas into a new business venture can appreciate the full extent of the risks involved and the weight that brings to bear on investors. In many instances, the risk to one's good name and self-esteem is greater than the risk of monetary loss.

Needless to say, neither Saint-Simon nor Karl Marx had ever opened a business.

The third was the constantly changing nature of the marketplace. What was in demand one moment was not in demand the next. The confiscation of industries assumed that what they were producing would always be in demand. It assumed that the marketplace was of a static nature, a fatal misunderstanding. The entrepreneur faces many challenges, not least of which is the success, or not, of his powers of prediction. The market is in a constant state of flux. Only the smartest and most fleet-of-foot entrepreneurs survive.

Though socialism was not practically established in the 19th century, its seeds of destruction for the 20th century were painstakingly developed. Soon after the industrial revolution began its creation of new wealth, the planning began to confiscate it. As always, there was no shortage of people with grand ideas about how to distribute the property of others.

> The object and the incitement of the nineteenth century was to accumulate wealth, while the duty of the twentieth century is the far more difficult task of securing its better distribution.
> Lord George Hamilton

It would have been instructive had Marx's theories been put into practice while money was still circulating. Without the ever-expanding debt of paper money, there would have been no time buffer to camouflage the results. The implementation of socialism under Gold would have seen the collapse of industries within weeks or months, not decades. It was the endless stream of paper money that put so much obfuscating time between the cause and its effects.

When a bridge collapses then accusing eyes turn toward the engineer. If a plane falls out of the sky on its first flight, either the designer or the builder is in serious trouble. With the economy, there has been no such connection between cause and effect. The time span between the implementation of modern economic theory and the subsequent collapse takes a few generations, sometimes longer. If the collapse were in the short-term then economists would be in trouble; the fact that the collapse takes so long seems to absolve them of responsibility.

———❧———

The Rise of Socialism

'Work, boys, work and be contented
So long as you've enough to buy a meal;
The man you may rely
Will be wealthy by and by
If he'll only put his shoulder to the wheel.'

Songs for English Workers—1867

While Marx's ideas were not wildly popular with workers; they aroused much interest elsewhere. Some of those with established and large businesses were none too keen on the growing struggle against the generation of agile entrepreneurs who had emerged from the ranks of former serfs and who now had access to bank loans. The gains in profit from falling production costs due to new technologies were being lost due to these cut-price competitors. The consuming public of course loved it, but from the vantage point of a well-padded boardroom chair the competition of the marketplace was unwelcome.

Growing government control of the economy had given an incentive for established businesses to form cosy relationships with regulators. This assured a strong influence regarding who was to run what were going to become highly regulated industries; monopolies in all but name. Marx's ideas were a godsend to entrenched business interests and regulators.

Capitalists would welcome any commercial reorganisation which would give them a calmer life. It is, we believe, not as a remedy for the miseries of the poor, but as an alleviation of the cares of the rich, that socialism is coming upon us.

Archdeacon Cunningham—1879

Archdeacon Cunningham's observation was astute, but the captains of industry were not the only people to prick their ears up at Marx's theories.

———∞∞∞———

Papers Please

The idea of 'top down control' resonated with governments throughout the world. What had begun in 1825, as the embryonic musings of Saint-Simon and his somewhat eccentric philosophical movement, had, less than 100 years later, become the template for international governance. Governments adopted, to one degree or another, the Saint-Simon/Marxist notion that their primary purpose was to control the economy and to guide the day-to-day activities of 'their' citizens.

Inducements were provided in the form of handouts to those who conformed to the new orthodoxy. In 1881, Otto Eduard Leopold von Bismarck, the inaugural Chancellor of the new German Empire was the first to formulate and implement state welfare. Memories of the French Revolution were disturbingly vivid and it was seen as a way of maintaining control over the newly emancipated German serfs. Employers and employees paid for the welfare, but, and most importantly, the government controlled it. The cleverness of the scheme was widely admired. Other governments seeking to further their own control imitated it.

'He who has his thumb on the purse has the power.'
Otto von Bismarck 21ˢᵗ May 1869

Emergency measures that had been put in place at the commencement of war in 1914 were never removed. It became impossible to cross national borders without a passport (a previously unknown concept outside Russia) and impossible to drive a car or open a business without a licence. In parts of Europe, one hundred years after World War One finished, moving house still requires registration with the police—'papers please.'

The serfs, who had been liberated by the accumulation and circulation of money in the 19th century, began their tragic journey back to serfdom in the 20th century. The State dictated standards and the citizens obeyed—or else. Incrementally, one little piece of legislation at a time, everything became forbidden unless specifically permitted. All governments became underpinned by the certainty of belief that, as a collective body, they held a superior wisdom to the people.

The withdrawal of money in 1914 brought to power, for the first time since the Divine Right of Kings, people wielding a justification for the repression of humanity. Prior to circulating Gold, they just did it when they could because they could. The international socialist movement gave those seeking total power over the lives of others what they had always craved, the veneer of intellectual respectability.

The combined application of socialism and paper money has contributed to human degradation and suffering in a severity of manner that has been without equal in the course of history.

Education

It is conventional wisdom that a prosperous economy is built upon an educated populace. This inspires governments to meddle even further in education. From this they believe will come production and prosperity—and taxes. An educated population is a result not a cause; it is what emerges when money accumulates and circulates.

Complex exchange creates a more complex society. A complex society requires more complex knowledge. The demand for more complex knowledge means that the value of knowledge rises and it becomes more desirable. If knowledge has little value then it will not be desired and will not happen to any great degree. Knowledge cannot be forced on people; if it is valuable they will desire it, if it is not then they will not. Knowledge has value in proportion to the perception of its applicability. A committed pastry cook does not take night classes in quantum mechanics.

Without circulating money there will be few investments or jobs. This in turn diminishes the value of education, while ensuring that there is insufficient revenue, either government tax or individual wage, to pay for it anyway. An education costs money. Schools do not get built for nothing; equipment does not get supplied for nothing and, like everyone else in the world, teachers do not wish to work for nothing.

A successful society does not rest upon education; an education rests upon the accumulation and circulation of money. Schools were begun in the private sector in response to the industrial revolution. New technologies required new skills. Industry realised that they could expand further and faster with a more educated workforce; parents realised that if their children were educated they could gain better jobs with higher wages.

The positive dynamics of money thrust outward in all directions. An educated population is one of the countless blessings that derive from the accumulation and circulation of Gold.

School curriculums, at least in the western world, now distort the history of the industrial revolution to the degree that Gold is not even mentioned.

———∞∞∞———

The stern dictates of Gold had imposed its own disciplines, not only on individuals, but, at least as importantly, on governments. The majority of people abided by its disciplines and lived free, decent, secure and social lives. Absent the disciplines of Gold, not only education, but morality, personal responsibility and even the concept of right and wrong began to break down. Lacking the honest exchange that can only come from honest money, society began its slow collapse.

———∞∞∞———

The Equality of Gold

Money ensures an equality of opportunity—for all people. That is one of the reasons that the ruling classes are so opposed to it. The circulation of money began the breakdown of the social segregation between those who were born into privilege, and those who were not. The clear lesson of 1500 BC, but which was not made evident until the 19th century AD, was that an artificial class system could not long survive under Gold. Money is the great leveller.

> The hope that poverty and ignorance may gradually be extinguished, derives indeed much support from the steady progress of the working classes during the nineteenth century.
> Alfred Marshall *Principles of Economics* 1890

With money in circulation, it is the productive who are rewarded, not the well connected. Once money is owned, whether by people saving for their children's education, their retirement years or an investment, it cannot be devalued. They can save with complete confidence that it will hold its value. People were able to make predictions and plans for the future with the security and certainty of Gold.

———

A Time for Change

Why is it important that we know how and why Gold became money and what money is?

The answer is that at the beginning of the 21st century the world is in crisis. While a few understand this, almost no one comprehends the cause. This has resulted in solutions being applied that were doomed to fail because they failed to address the underlying problem. The crisis is a credit crisis brought about by the abandonment of money and the use of paper money in its stead. This impediment to honest exchange has been exacerbated by social decay stemming from the same cause. The adoption and application of Saint Simon inspired Marxist theories of top down control and redistribution of wealth was rank icing atop an already rotting paper cake.

An understanding of the true nature of the current crisis presents predictions. They are grim. We have had currency crisis before, but not worldwide. The globalisation of the latter part of the 20th century locked emerging economies into the fate of the larger nations. The unstable paper monies of the world are entangled in a grand debt alliance that sees nations' foreign reserves held in the paper money of other nations. The contamination factor will be one hundred per cent. This is not just Europe and the Anglos; the whole world is in crisis.

During the Great Depression of the 1930s, many returned to the home farms. Few prospered, but most survived. There are not many home farms to return to in the western world of the 21st century. When the money breaks down, the food supply chain will soon follow. There will be problems of an unprecedented nature. Compounding that will be the situation of 'just in time' delivery. All businesses, including food retailing, are conducted on the basis that only a few days stock at normal trading volumes are kept in store. When panic hits, the shelves will be empty within hours. How long will it be before they are refilled?

On top of all this will be layered the moral degeneration created by one hundred years of disfigured exchange. The 'right' to something for nothing will not vanish overnight. When the government ceases to provide the 'something', it will be sought elsewhere; it is after all an entitlement. The construction of a society is a work of art; its destruction rings a less aesthetic note.

If government retreats, which is possible in the general chaos of a complete monetary collapse, then the recovery will be painful, but swift. The free market will swing into action as it always does when not constrained. Food, water, energy and basic services will be quickly restored.

If government refuses to retreat, then people will die in large numbers and the disaster will be prolonged. Unless we change direction, one of those scenarios is our future.

The collapse of society is unlikely to turn on light bulbs. Scapegoats will be sought and found. As in all other ages and in similar, though not as severe situations, migrants (outsiders) will be targeted; particularly those who look, speak, dress or act differently. An already disastrous situation will become even uglier. Those who predicted and made plans accordingly will also be victims of the witch-hunt. The words 'profiteer'; 'speculator' and 'hoarder' will again be used by the dull and unimaginative to persecute the more prescient.

The width between 'haves' and 'have-nots' is not a neutral, statistical void; it is the gulf between two vastly differing points of view. Those differing realities will have as their ultimate manifestation mutual hatred; it will come in the guise of superiors and inferiors. The seeds are again being sown for the re-emergence of lords and serfs. Soon will come the attempt at an intellectual justification for such an outcome; then will come the new laws.

Law making is no longer concerned with the maintenance of individual rights; it is about the maintenance of the collective status quo. If, despite that, the status quo changes, as is happening now, then the laws will be re-written to validate that change and lords and serfs will become the new legal reality.

—————⊗⊗⊗—————

How have we survived so long without Gold? The answer is that we have squandered the accumulated capital of the centuries. The wealthier nations delayed the inevitable by encouraging immigrants and greater 'workforce participation' which increased their taxation base. Then the borrowing accelerator pedal, already held down firmly, was pushed to the floor. Borrowings have reached such gigantic levels that even the interest cannot be serviced, never mind the capital. We have reached the bottom of the barrel. The scenario could not be bleaker.

The consumption of the capital of the past, present and future is grinding to a halt—it has mostly gone. Falling interest rates, on top of increasing regulation and compliance costs, have almost destroyed the potential for legal wealth creation. Taxation has so far played a severe, but lesser role. That will change. The fall in the creation of new businesses due to a lack of enough incentive to offset the hurdles will accelerate.

Knowing what money is means that it can be known what money is not. The use of paper money, in conjunction with top down theories of market control, has led the world into a very strange and dangerous place. People's natural urge to produce and exchange has been stymied. Complex exchange, and thus society, is on the verge of complete breakdown.

The Future of Western Society

While the whole world is affected, some parts will be impacted more than others. The Anglo world and Europe are exhausted; they have run their course. The weight of paper money and government regulation around its neck has proved too great. The gap between rich and poor is wider than at any point since the early 19th century. Intellectually the west is demoralized, effete and degenerate. It endures, without momentum or purpose, kept in existence only by complacency and inertia. Self-reliance has given way to self-pity.

Welfare recipients occupy one end of the spectrum of existence; paper-shuffling financiers, bankers, public servants and politicians the other. The size of both is growing. In between are the crushed, demoralized and dwindling remnants of the productive—the wealth producers. The life spirit, the élan vital of western society, is departing—not with a bang, nor even a whimper; it is just imperceptibly drifting off into the shadows.

Society requires not only diffused accumulations of money and its widespread circulation; but also people who are hungry for survival to take advantage of it. The reintroduction of money to western society now might not act as the spark that many hope. Maybe the degeneration has gone too far—survival is assumed, no longer worked for. If that is true, either the degenerate will die out in the paper money grand finale, or the genetic stock of the west will be enhanced by invasion of a more survival-orientated people. A combination of the two is the historical norm. War is resorted to and the degenerate, bred for nothing but conflict, are sent off to be slaughtered. They go willingly, and likely ineffectively, against a more vigourous and intelligent people.

Other cultures are watching the withering away of western society—not with indifference, but with a sense of Shadenfreude, based on both real and imagined past injustices.

Many in the western world have morally deteriorated to the point where they are not even aware that they are responsible for their own survival. Their weekly reality is free paper money—paper money for no exchange. Situations of total dependency have existed in previous ages, but with a difference. Former slaves or serfs had economic value to their masters, which meant that there was a reasonable likelihood they would be looked after, at least sufficient to maintain their productivity. They tilled fields, gathered crops, cooked meals and cleaned houses.

They were of use.

Welfare serfs have no economic value; quite the reverse, they have adopted their submissive lifestyle willingly and have a minus economic value. Their modern day lord and master, the government, will have no hesitation in abandoning them at the first sign of economic distress. At the point where democracy has collapsed and martial law is in place, votes have zero market value.

A transition from our current malaise to a Golden future is still technically possible, but time is running out.

Chapter Twenty-six
When Gold Speaks

Auro loquente omnis oratio inanis est.
(When Gold speaks, the world is silent and listens.)

The glory of Gold has not just paralleled humanity's progress; it has to the greatest degree, inspired and formed it. Such a contribution cannot be brushed aside without severe consequences. Gold bears the weight of being the only money with dignity and grace, but a proper understanding cannot be restricted to its workaday functions. Gold was the anvil upon which the modern world was forged, not just monetary but also intellectually.

Gold devolved from its Supreme Being spiritual status to become the supreme commodity of the material universe. It was through the auspices of Gold that humanity evolved from its primitive state. Gold has mined man just as thoroughly as man has mined Gold. We have overlooked its importance in the manner of the dandelion that fails to intellectually note the importance of rain. We have sensed its mystique at a deep, primal level, but failed to recognise its true stature. That arrogance, for such it is, has cost us dearly in the past, and now hangs over society like a pall. It is only the acknowledgment of Gold's unique role in humanity's past that will ensure our future survival as social beings. We are the children of Gold.

Humanity has tended to assume a linear progression as the natural human state. There is no evidence for this. Life does not automatically progress, one little incremental step at a time. The tendency of humanity is not toward innovation; it is toward continuation at a low level of existence. For millennia after millennia humanity plodded on doing the same old things in the same old ways. The changes ranged from minimal to non-existent. For hundreds of thousands of years humans used pointy sticks and stone hammers as their most sophisticated tools. It was only the emergence of Gold that changed this.

After unknown further millennia, Gold entered the marketplace as money. This was the harbinger of real change—the production of surplus goods brought about by the ability to store, transport, measure and exchange a precise commercial value. It was this that led to innovation and further advancement.

Our ancient forebears were not ignorant or lacking skills, as evidenced by the exquisite cave paintings dating from Palaeolithic times. Such creative and sensitive displays were not enough to stop them from starving to death and being killed by the cold, wild animals and disease. Egypt circa 1500 BC was the evolutionary leap. Ways of life that had existed for tens of thousands of years were swept aside in an instant. The grand entrance of money was a sudden and extraordinary lurch into a new dimension. Were it not for the worship of the Sun God and the association of Gold with the solar deity, then the best that humanity could have achieved would have been a cumbersome credit arrangement using wheat or salt or some other trade good.

Gold can again join together the disparate cultures. Without it, the world is reduced to tribes seeking gain, not by production, but by looting the wealth of others. The commonality and unity evidenced by Gold becomes, in its absence, overshadowed by the superficial differences. It is under such circumstances that the evil and stupid lead people to war. We have so much taken money for granted that we have failed to grasp not only its significance, but also the wondrous realm that it bestowed upon us.

Gold changed the human world from a monotonous, drab and dangerous existence, where every day was a life and death struggle for survival, into a kaleidoscope of previously unimaginable opportunities and possibilities. Without the extraordinary occurrence of the alignment of Gold's value with the values ascribed to the Sun God, the world would have had no money.

Lacking the unique circumstances that gave rise to money, life in the 21st century would be no different than it was pre 1500 BC. Money changed the history of the world or, more precisely, it gave flower to the latent human ingenuity that changed the history of the world. Unless we again rise to the necessary level of awareness, the absence of money will change it again. The passage of time did not create human advancement; it was the emergence of a store of stable value and the subsequent development of its roles in the marketplace that allowed for that.

It was only for a short blip in the aeon of humanity's existence that Gold was utilized in the marketplace—less than three and a half thousand years out of hundreds of thousands. It was only in that brief interval that we intermittently tasted the concepts of prosperity and the freedom of the individual. A future without money in the marketplace is a grim prospect for our descendants and a sad indictment of the heights of folly of the current age.

For 3,500 years, grand societies have risen then collapsed and the cause has been construed as a complete mystery to one and all. All sorts of guesses have been offered, including moral degeneracy and the loss of a sense of duty. The real reason, called loudly and unequivocally from the pages of history, is that time after time, society after society, governments of all brands have cheated people by abusing their monopoly control of the money.

> The vanishing of gold coins from circulation has historically been followed by a collapse of trade if not immediately, then certainly in a century or so.
>
> Professor Antal E. Fekete

—❧—

In the 20th and 21st centuries we have been burdened by the grand delusion that we are smarter than people who lived in prior ages; the dazzle of technology has blinded us. Linguistically and monetarily, and thus socially, humanity is at a low point. The two primary forms of exchange have been eviscerated. What remains of social cohesion exists courtesy of an ever more aggressively intrusive State. History teaches that accelerating social fragmentation cannot be halted for long by repression. The unifying factors of Gold and language are the key to reversing this social spiral. As there can be no comparable substitute for language in the exchange of ideas, so there can be no comparable substitute for money in the exchange of goods.

It is possible that the final act to our current monetary theatre will see new paper monies introduced that are 'backed' by Gold. Another paper standard may work for a while, and it may not. What is certain is that the later it is left, the harder it will be to convince people that this new paper will be any better than previous paper. Paper that is not redeemable for Gold is still just paper. Once paper money collapses, it takes a few generations for the people to lose the memory of the resultant hardships and to regain their misplaced trust in government controlled credit systems.

The money of the world is Gold; it always has been and it always will be, because it is the only money possible. The lack of an understanding of this has brought societies to the brink. If we lose our money, then we lose our all. To suggest that the understanding of money is more important than most people give it credit for is the understatement of history.

By 2009, the Zimbabwean Prime Minister Robert Mugabe and his finance minister Gideon Gono had degraded the Zimbabwe paper dollar to the point where it collapsed. It is doubtful that many of the Zimbabwe villagers had degrees in the monetary science, yet within weeks, Gold had re-emerged in the marketplace as the only acceptable money (a loaf of bread cost 0.01grams). The old banknotes still had a valuable part to play; they were used as wrapping paper for money.

This example provides great encouragement for the future. It does not require a degree in economics to know that a known weight and fineness of Gold is money. On the contrary, at the start of the 21st century with the subject of economics in utter disrepute, one could be forgiven for believing that you needed a degree in economics to not understand it.

The first people to introduce the Gold standard will form the next great society. Nothing else matters; nothing else is of the same fundamental importance. The rest of the world will follow, just as England's introduction of Gold in the 18th century led the world back to Gold in the 19th century.

No society has long survived its severance from money. Without the reintroduction of Gold, the world will return to a not-so-distant past (relative to the whole span of humanity) that will be unimaginably hard. Those individuals who hoard Gold and silver, and imagine that they can ride out the tough times, need to be warned against complacency. Some believe that when the current monetary system collapses, all will still be the same except that they will be the new rich. That is preposterously naïve.

Is there enough Gold to use it as money throughout the whole world? Yes, there is more than enough. Is there enough money for governments to continue to fight interminable wars, or fund ever more imaginative and expensive welfare schemes in order to retain their grip on power? No, fortunately there will never be enough money for that.

———⊶⊷———

Not much stress has been laid in the book on history's successful examples of using Gold as money. This is for the reason that, for those prepared to look, they are too obvious and numerous to mention. The breathtakingly beautiful European cities of Vienna, Budapest, Prague and Venice, amongst many others, stand as living testaments to the prosperity and quality of life that accompanies the circulation of Gold. Their mere presence speaks more eloquently than this author ever could.

One hundred years ago there were many other cities that could have been placed in the same category, but they were destroyed in the paper money wars of the 20th century. Yet it is more than just the beautiful architecture that catches the breath; it is what was created within those edifices. The stroke of Gold's delicate brush dabbed on life's canvas brought glory to the full spectrum of human activity; from the humdrum yet vital area of its monetary use, across the arts, music, literature, education, morality and spirituality.

Only the idle, and those who suffer from the delusion that they are born to rule over others (usually one and the same), have reason to fear and denigrate Gold. The successful machinations of these paper-intellectuals are the reason for today's extreme wealth gap between the 'haves' and the 'have-nots'.

The commonality of humanity still exists, just as it has always done. The difference is that we have lost sight of it, to the same degree that we have lost sight of Gold. It is imperative that we rediscover the basic truth of our distant ancestors, before we lose the foundation of society that they bequeathed us. Gold is the glue that binds us, one to the other. Attempts to remove that influence are of the same order of magnitude as trying to remove the core elements of consciousness. To resist Gold is to resist the forces of survival and our rightful place in this universe.

It is a dark time that we are living through and it will soon become darker, but that darkness will again be pierced by the dawn of Gold. For thus it has always been and always will be, for both life and Gold are eternal. With the blessings of Gold, alongside its adjunct silver, there is no good reason for this planet to be other than a Garden of Eden. From King Croesus of Lydia in 560 BC, right down to the present day, the only thing that has kept humanity in shortage instead of plenty, in war instead of peace, in misery instead of happiness and under surveillance instead of freedom, is government control of money.

The odd thing is that this observation will, to some, be regarded as contentious, or even extreme. It is not either. In light of the unveiling of the real story of money it is a statement of the obvious. That Gold is the only money is one of those facts that do not cease to exist simply because it is ignored. It is not money that is failing; money retreated into hoards and has continued to heroically perform its role as the store of stable value. It is the paper monies, forced upon the marketplace by governments, which are failing.

Soon the stormy clouds will blow over and both Gold and humanity will emerge into the bright light of the Sun and a new Golden age. The optimism born of Gold, together with its beauty, practicality and peerless honesty, will be a revelation.

> 'There is a tide in the affairs of men.
> Which, taken at the flood, leads on to fortune;
> Omitted, all the voyage of their life
> Is bound in shallows and in miseries.
> On such a full sea are we now afloat,
> And we must take the current when it serves,
> Or lose our ventures.'
> William Shakespeare—*Julius Caesar*, Act 4, scene 3

The End

Summary

1. Gold's stability of value was formed outside the marketplace.
2. Circa 1500 BC, Gold's stability of value migrated to the marketplace.
3. Because Gold is a stable value it is the measure of value.
4. Only the measure of value can be money.
5. The most influential monetary factor comes not from transactions, but from accumulations.
6. Only Gold can be accumulated with the certainty of full value retention.
7. An understanding of the real origins of money explains its 'mysterious' relationship with silver.
8. Government monopolisation of money has been reliably destructive.
9. The study of economics and money has been deeply flawed.
10. It is time for change before we go over the cliff.

Definitions

It was in the search for precise definitions in the study of money, and in the discovery that there were few that made any sense, that my curiosity was first piqued. How could there be a so-called science that could not define its terms—that could not even define the subject?

Gold:	A store of stable value*
Money:	A known weight and fineness of Gold
Surrogate money:	A known weight and fineness of silver
Good (noun):	An exchangeable, quantifiable value
Trade good:	An easily exchangeable good used to transfer value into the future
Medium of exchange:	A trade good
Most marketable good:	The trade good perceived to have the most stability of value
Paper money:	A token trade good
The Gold Standard:	The use of money or its silver surrogate as the only measure of value
Complex exchange	The high degree of human interaction brought about by circulating money.
Society:	An enduring state of harmonious, widespread and complex exchange

* Marketplace definition only

AFTERWORD

*How easily the learned give up the evidence of their senses to
preserve the coherence of the ideas in their imagination.*

Adam Smith

It was one simple question: 'what is the definition of money?' and my inability to find a credible answer, even from my learned professor, that led to this book and the fascinating journey that it became.

What a strange species we are that a whole 'science' was built up around such a fundamentally flawed concept. I am well aware that entrenched views and the pride of lofty position are not overcome by mere logic and common sense. The feeling of foreboding that comes from that is less commanding than the urge, no, the necessity and responsibility, to publish and be damned. I take full responsibility for the central theme of the book; to my knowledge, at the point of writing they are not the views of anyone else and nor have they ever been.

I acknowledge the controversial nature of what is written. Will there be mistakes here and there? Probably, the logic demanded that I dip my toe into a multitude of areas where I had little to no prior knowledge. In particular the dates ascribed to specific societies and reigns in the ancient world vary quite a bit. As it was not crucial to the story, I acknowledge that I used those that seemed the most accepted.

Am I confident of the overall correctness of the book's conclusions? Absolutely, when the jigsaw is assembled and all the pieces fit together and the picture displayed is complete, consistent and coherent, the validity of the result cannot be in question. The definition and roles of money are not presented as possibility, but as fact. The subject of money has been an almost total foul up from beginning to end—headless chickens laying cracked monetary theories and no one knowing what came first. Economics is not at all complicated—ask any manager of the household budget. What is valid at that level is equally valid in the aggregate.

There is of course far more to the complete story of money than is touched upon in this book. Even the areas that I have touched upon need fleshing out. It had to end somewhere. Nevertheless, it is a sound grounding in the subject and puts to the sword the major confusions and errors that have left the subject rather bogged to this point.

From our current perspective Gold seems to have been around 'forever'. In truth we have had our money for only a fraction of humanity's history. There can be little doubt that humanity will learn how to take full advantage of Gold's blessings at some point. Will that be now, or in another 100 or 1000 years? Only time can answer that question.

Philip Barton October 2014

He has not lived who gathers gold,
Nor has he lived whose life is told
In selfish battles he has won,
Or deed of skill that he has done,
But he has lived who now and then
Has helped along his fellowman.

Edgar Albert Guest

Addendum
The Myths of Gold

*Thinking to get at once all the gold the goose could give, he
killed it and opened it only to find—nothing.*

Aesop's Fables

Much of this addendum will be unnecessary for the attentive reader.
Once Gold's origins and its subsequent transition to the marketplace are
understood, the errors contained in the myths become easy to spot. Should
there be any residual confusion on the subject then this section should help
lay them to rest.

After its abandonment by governments in 1914 (later in the US and
Switzerland), Gold suffered from decades of bad press. Whilst genuine
ignorance of Gold's significance was in play, this was compounded by a
policy of deliberate disinformation. For reasons of perceived self-interest,
governments had removed money from circulation and embarked on a
worldwide experiment utilising paper money. They needed to rationalise
and justify their actions.

There are doubtless other residuals of the propaganda that was
designed to denigrate money, but the following are the most commonly
encountered.

There is not enough Gold ...

The British Empire at its peak was a huge, worldwide commercial operation. It operated on 150—200 tonnes of Gold. The world now has at least 171 *thousand* tonnes of Gold. Should one be under the misapprehension that trade is greater these days, then bear in mind that the highly globalized period of the 1870s to the start of the First World War in 1914 produced annual volumes of world trade that were not exceeded until the early 1970s.

The key to the survival of our great societies is Gold; not only accumulating, but also circulating. A move toward a Gold standard does not involve returning to Gold as money; Gold has never stopped being money. What moving forward to a Gold standard means is the drawing out of Gold from the hoards. The degree that Gold is hoarded is highly correlated to the degree that governments are not trusted. When governments are honest and transparent, Gold circulates. In the best possible world, all Gold would be in circulation. Conversely, in the worst possible world all Gold would be in hiding. It is instructive to ponder on where all Gold is right now.

When Gold is in hiding it can seem that there is not much of it. When a government official or a central banker speaks of there 'not being enough Gold to return it to its monetary status', then you know that the person doing the talking is a part of the reason Gold seems in short supply.

Gold is never in short supply, except when for good reason it is being hoarded. There are three reasons for hoarding, all of them valid. The first is the need to provide insurance for the lean times such as old age or infirmity. The second is to accumulate capital for investment. The third is as a safe haven against the ravages of paper money or adulterated coins.

Possibly the most egregious lie, for it needs to be plainly stated that that is what this myth is, was that Gold had to be withdrawn from circulation because the economy was so strong that there was not enough Gold to service it, which resulted in deflation. Yes, prices were falling, but that will always happen in a healthy economy. The falling prices were due to improving technologies and competition of the free market. That will always ensure falling prices. Who could sensibly object to that?

There is too much Gold ...

This myth is not as common now as it was when Gold was circulating during the 19th century. It is worth covering though as it may return along with the circulation of Gold.

Despite the relative success of the classical Gold standard, it would be an error to assume that there existed a better knowledge of Gold then than in the 20th or early 21st century. As recently as the 16th century the belief still existed in Europe that it was the Sun's rays striking mud that created Gold. The knowledge that Gold was money was accepted without question, however the reason this was so was absent; a situation that has remained undisturbed up to the present.

Around 1820, the legendary Russian Gold of the Ural Mountains, made famous by the writings of Herodotus, began again to flow (silver also). From small beginnings, by 1830 the rediscovered Russian Gold fields were officially producing 5.78 tonnes of Gold a year. Then the Siberian Gold fields opened up.

> About this time (1830) the auriferous deposits of Siberia became known, and from 1840 they yielded a far greater mass of gold than that extracted from the mines of the Oural.
>
> Michel Chevalier

In late 1848, Gold was discovered in California. By 1849 miners were pouring in and Gold began pouring out. In 1851, Gold was discovered in Australia; first New South Wales and then Victoria. Discoveries in Canada, New Zealand, South Africa and Alaska followed.

The rising volume of new Gold reaching the market in the mid 19th century was matched by an accompanying concern. It reached a peak in 1859 when Michel Chevalier, a professor of political economy at the College de France and Member of the Institute de France, published a book entitled *On the Probable Fall in the Value of Gold*. It was translated into English in the same year by Richard Cobden* and published in England and Scotland. The book went into three printings in Britain alone. In modern parlance 'it went viral'.

> 'Under the influence of this greatly increased and cheapened production of gold, it is reasonable to expect, at least in all those countries where gold circulates in large quantities, and where it is or tends to be the sole medium of exchange, a general disturbance of prices ...'
>
> Michel Chevalier

London, the world's financial centre, had already received large amounts of the new Gold and, according to Chevalier, should expect to receive even more, probably around 50% of the new Gold in total. According to subsequent reports, about 80% of the Australian Gold made its way to England, and about 20% of the Californian Gold. Chevalier predicted that the quantity of new Gold coming into the market would cause Gold's value to fall and that this would bring about increases in the price of goods across the board. The bankers became as agitated as was possible in the staid world of 19th century British banking. They regarded stable commodity prices as a primary factor in Britain's industrial prosperity.

Chevalier's book led to wild speculations throughout Europe as to the future course of markets. In the event, Gold confounded the 19th century pundits in the same manner that it had confounded them before and has

---

*   Richard Cobden and Michel Chevalier were the inspirations for the Cobden-Chevalier Treaty signed by England and France in 1860. The treaty successfully advanced the idea and practise of trade between the two nations, instead of war.

continued to since. It maintained the stable value that it had held for the prior thousands of years. Despite all the new Gold entering the market, prices of most goods continued the general downward trend exhibited under Gold in both the UK and the US for most of the 19th century. The imagined crisis passed and was soon forgotten by history ... along with its important lesson.

The notion that additional Gold arriving into the marketplace would cause instability in the monetary system was derived from the erroneous belief that Gold was a good that was priced in pounds: more supply equals less demand equals prices fall. This cart pulling the horse economics was the basis of Chevalier's concerns. Knowledge of the stock-to-flow and its importance was lacking. Couple that with the lack of a definition for money and the breeding ground for confusion was fertile.

It was not realised that Gold does not have a declining marginal utility; that it was not a good that suffers a drop in value the more one has of it. The root cause of the confusion however was the lack of understanding of Gold's stability of value and its origins.

You cannot eat Gold ...

That is a fact. The nutritional qualities of paper, plastic, zinc and seashells are also highly suspect. The role of money is not to be eaten[**].

Without paper money, governments would not be able to inject liquidity into the system via their central banks ...

The world is awash with such a volume of government created liquidity (debt) that it can never be repaid. The first priority to fixing the terrible mess that the world is in is to abort the ability of governments and central banks to create 'liquidity'. With the Gold standard, self-liquidating bills of exchange provide all the liquidity that is needed.

[**]   Of interest is that the bacterium Delftia acidovorans does eat Gold. It dines on water-soluble Gold and excretes tiny nuggets. That a genetically modified variant of this Gold-eating, nugget-layer will eventually be harnessed to mine the oceans (bio-mineralisation) seems plausible.

A modern economy is too complicated for Gold ...

A modern economy appears to be complicated because we have been attempting to use paper instead of money. The economy looked just as complicated to the Chinese one thousand years ago when they were experimenting with the first paper money system. The electronic era coupled with circulating money will simplify the economy. Everyone will benefit from that except the vast numbers of financiers, investment advisers, lawyers and accountants that the complicated nature of the current system requires. Under the Gold standard, when bankers and economists opened their mouths, normal people would understand what they were talking about.

The world of Gold is an uncomplicated world of rising production, and rising wealth and savings for working people. It is not a world of unlimited political power and unspeakably huge and unearned bonuses for financiers and bankers. That is why politicians, financiers and bankers, along with their in-house economists, are the shrillest voices denouncing Gold.

The Great Depression was caused by Gold ...

The 1920s stock market and real estate boom was called 'The Roaring Twenties' and was made possible by the same mechanism as 'The New Era' boom of the 1990s ... Federal Reserve Bank induced easy credit utilising interest rates that were too low. In 1929, when it was no longer possible to expand credit, the boom collapsed and deflation took over. As it would be described these days ... the bubble burst.

The best way to stop a bubble from bursting is to not blow one up in the first place.

Despite having the same culprit, there are some significant differences between the Great Depression of the 1930s and the current situation:

a.   this time, because there is no Gold constraint at all, the credit expansion has been much larger than in the 1920s. Consequently, the resultant debt collapse will be much worse.

b. this time, due to the interlinked nature of currencies, the problem will be worldwide.

c. this time the central bankers won't be able to blame Gold.

The Gold standard is for the rich ...

The last time people used Gold as money was in the 19th century. It was not the Gold standard, as much of the paper in circulation was un-backed by Gold, but it was still an era of unprecedented rising prosperity for working people.

Only 'in the know' speculators, bankers, sharp operators and politicians gain from government-issued paper representations of money. Productive people and pensioners can only lose over the longer term.

Many people have no Gold and would be disadvantaged ...

Many people in the present, despite having produced all their working lives, have no paper money and are already disadvantaged. Under the Gold standard they would earn real money that kept its value.

Countries with a lot of Gold would have an unfair advantage ...

It has always cost approximately one ounce of Gold to mine one ounce of Gold. That is why having a lot of Gold in the ground has rarely made a country, a company or an individual rich. Gold mining has always run on a very fine profit margin.

Gold flows towards those who produce and trade and away from those that do not. Today, China is the largest producer and trader of goods and the largest saver, for that reason it is also the largest importer of Gold. It is Gold on the move through trade that makes a country rich, not Gold in the ground.

Those countries and people who work and produce valuable and exchangeable goods acquire Gold. Where it comes from is irrelevant. A country with a large existing Gold stock but no Gold income is in a dangerous position. A country with no Gold stock but a Gold income will do just fine.

The price movement of Gold makes it too volatile to be money ...

When people talk about the 'price' of Gold, they have it the wrong way round. What they mean is the price of the paper money that is measured by (valued in) Gold. Gold is the measure, not the measured. All sciences consist of that which measures and that which is measured; the monetary science is no different. In the monetary science the measure is Gold. Paper monies are very volatile in value; Gold is stable. When people see the 'price of Gold' go up, what they are witnessing is the fall in the value of paper money—as measured by Gold.

Imagine sitting on the beach as the tide drops and exposes a rock. As the tide recedes ever further the rock becomes more and more exposed. We do not say: 'look how high that rock is going up'. We more sensibly say: 'look how low the water is dropping'. So it is with the rock of Gold. It is not the value of Gold that is going up, it is the value of the paper money that is dropping.

It should be clear by now that a proper understanding of money requires the dismissal of almost all prior assumptions. Anyone who talks about the 'price of Gold' is expressing a fundamental misunderstanding. Much as governments and modern economists would love there to be a 'price of Gold', it is not possible. An unstable value cannot be used to measure the stable value.

When you see a graph showing the rise in the 'price of Gold'. Turn it upside down and back-to-front. Then you will see through the back of the paper what is really being measured ... the collapsing value of paper money, or, looked at another way, the collapsing state of societies. Gold is not an investment as it will never make anybody money; how could it, it is already money. Gold's job is as a store of stable value. It will transition wealth from the here and now, to wherever it is that we end up when this current paper money experiment breaks down.

Gold is deflationary ...

To deflate the money supply it would have to be poked back down into the geological strata of a Gold mine. That is a nonsensical concept.

When this myth is referring to prices, then it is a fact that in the 19th century, in both the UK and the US, prices fell for almost the entire period. This was at a time when the quality of goods was improving. Imagine a scenario where the economy and wages are growing, and where simultaneously the weekly working hours are falling, and where each unit of money is able to buy more and more of better quality goods as time goes on. That is how it was in the 19th century and how it should be in a healthy economy. Under a system of honest money, rising productivity and technical innovation will always lead to a gradual fall in the overall price of goods.

Gold and silver coins are too heavy to use as money ...

During the Weimar Republic people found it easier and lighter to carry a tiny silver coin than the wheelbarrow loads of its paper money equivalent.

At the time of writing, one ounce of Gold buys 1,674.50 Australian dollars. The notes and coin (in the largest denominations possible) are almost 19% heavier than the ounce of Gold. In the more normally carried denominations they are almost 70% heavier.

Legal tender is usually heavier and always bulkier than Gold. It is true that paper money is used for convenience, but it is not for the convenience of people, it is for the convenience of governments.

Gold is just another commodity ...

Gold is money as proven by 3,500 years of history and the stock-to-flow ratio. Commodities tend to be very volatile in value; Gold is stable in value—that is why it is the measure. To imagine that Gold is just another commodity is to imagine that the Koh-I-Noor diamond is just another piece of coal.

The myths of Gold do not take long to dispense with. Though it is easy and fast to construct and disseminate misinformation; it is always easier and faster to demolish it. Truth resonates.